John Dunmore Lang

**Origin and Migrations of the Polynesian Nation**

John Dunmore Lang

**Origin and Migrations of the Polynesian Nation**

ISBN/EAN: 9783337401894

Printed in Europe, USA, Canada, Australia, Japan

Cover: Foto ©ninafisch / pixelio.de

More available books at **www.hansebooks.com**

# ORIGIN AND MIGRATIONS

## OF THE

# POLYNESIAN NATION:

DEMONSTRATING

THEIR ORIGINAL DISCOVERY AND PROGRESSIVE
SETTLEMENT OF THE

CONTINENT OF AMERICA.

BY

JOHN DUNMORE LANG, D.D., A.M.

SENIOR MINISTER OF THE SCOTS CHURCH, SYDNEY, ETC.

**SECOND EDITION. GREATLY EXTENDED AND IMPROVED.**

GEORGE ROBERTSON,
SYDNEY, MELBOURNE, AND ADELAIDE.
MDCCCLXXVII.

# CONTENTS.

|  | PAGE. |
|---|---|
| Introduction ... ... ... ... | vii. |

### Chapter I.

✗ How the Polynesian Nation came to be spread over the numberless islands of the Pacific Ocean ... ... ... ... ... ... 1

### Chapter II.

✗ From what part of the world has the Polynesian Nation originally sprung; and with what part of the human family does it bear the strongest relations? ... ... 25

### Chapter III.

✗ At what period in the history of mankind did the separation of the Polynesian from the Malayan nation take place? ... ... 54

### Chapter IV.

✗ What course the forefathers of the Polynesian Nation must, in all likelihood, have taken, in their voyages to the eastward, across the Pacific Ocean ... ... 74

iv.

## Chapter V.

✗ The westerly winds that had propelled the forefathers of the Polynesian Nation from their original starting point, in the Philippine Islands, to their farthest east, in Easter Island — a distance of upwards of seven thousand miles, across the broadest part of the Pacific Ocean—must have carried them across the remaining narrow tract of ocean to the American land, and given its first inhabitants to America ... ... 94

## Chapter VI.

Unity or identity of the Indo-American race from Labrador and the Lakes of Canada to Tierra del Fuego and Cape Horn ... 111

## Chapter VII.

✗ The Indo-Americans and Polynesians are one and the same people, sprung from the same primitive stock, and connected with each other by the mutual ties of parentage and descent ... ... ... ... ... ... 139

## Chapter VIII.

✗ There is no evidence, and not the slightest probability, of any emigration having ever taken place from Asia to America by Behring's Straits ... ... ... ... ... 187

## Chapter IX.

PAGE.

✗ There is no valid objection against the theory of this work, from the phenomena of language in America ... ... ... ... 224

## Chapter X.

✗ The Indo-Americans are not Aborigines in the sense of being a distinct creation from the rest of mankind, but are related, in the way of natural descent, to another large division of the family of man ... ... 266

## Chapter XI.

Resumé—Plagiarism extraordinary—Conclusion  298

# INTRODUCTION.

My attention happened to be strongly directed to the investigations which the subject of this volume implies, shortly after my arrival in New South Wales for the first time, upwards of fifty years ago, and I pursued them from time to time, as I had opportunity, both in the colony and more especially on my repeated voyages across the Southern Pacific Ocean, from Sydney to London, by Cape Horn. My enquiries were directed chiefly to ascertain the manner in which the islands of the South Seas had been originally peopled, and whether there was any affinity between the languages and the institutions and customs of their singular inhabitants and those o any other known division of the family of man.

I was induced to enter on this particular branch of literary and philosophical enquiry partly from a natural fondness for such investigations, but chiefly from the growing importance of the South Sea Islands, both as a field for missionary labour and for mercantile speculation, from the rapidly-extending connexion between several of the groups of these islands and the colony of New South Wales, and from the progress that was making at a comparatively early period in the colonization of the southernmost of the Polynesian groups — the island of New Zealand—by adventurers from that colony.

In pursuing these investigations, especially at sea, I had little else to refer to than the result of my own previous reading and observations, in the shape of a variety of unconnected *notanda* which I had made in the colony, some of which were extracts of works which I had previously read, while others were merely the details of facts relative to the South Sea Islands, of which I had been incidentally apprised during my residence in New South Wales.

In these investigations I had satisfied myself, after ten years residence in that colony, that the

Polynesians, or South Sea Islanders, were of Asiatic origin and Malayan race, and that, in the earliest period in the history of mankind, their forefathers had crossed, or rather been driven across by adverse winds, from the Indian Archipelago into the Western Pacific; and that from thence they had, in numberless ages past, not only peopled the multitude of the isles of that vast ocean, but had actually traversed almost its whole extent, to Easter Island, the farthest eastern limit of Captain Cook's discoveries in the Southern Pacific, that is, upwards of 7000 miles from their supposed point of departure, the Indian Archipelago.

This, I conceived at the time, was a great and important discovery; for no previous effort had ever been made, either to identify the Polynesians with the Malays, or to trace their subsequent history and migrations. In pursuing my investigations I found that the great difficulty that uniformly presented itself to writers of eminence on the Pacific Ocean and the Polynesians was the uniform prevalence of the easterly trade winds in the intertropical regions of that ocean; and as these winds, as was strongly maintained, would effectually prevent the South Sea Islanders from traversing the Pacific to the eastward, a learned Spaniard, the author of a history of the Philippine Islands, had advanced the singular theory—which Mr. Ellis, the author of a well-known and very able work, entitled " Polynesian Researches," had advocated and long maintained—that the South Sea Islands were originally discovered and settled from the West Coast of America. At length, however, I discovered, in continuation of my enquiries, that, from the testimony of that illustrious navigator, La Perouse, and another eminent English navigator—Captain, afterwards Admiral Hunter, the second Governor of New South Wales—there was a belt of ocean in the Pacific in which it was quite as practicable, at certain seasons, to sail to the eastward as to the westward. This discovery, which I afterwards announced, as I shall shew presently, was immediately adopted as the solution of this great problem by Mr. Ellis, who from that period renounced his own theory of the discovery and settlement of the South Sea Islands from the West Coast of America.

There was yet, however, a still greater discovery which Divine Providence had enabled me to make in the boundless Pacific Ocean — that of the way in which America had been originally discovered and progressively settled, by Polynesians from Easter Island crossing the intervening tract of ocean, of about 2000 miles, under a sudden and violent tempest of westerly wind, such as are frequent in the Southern Pacific, and such as I had experienced myself in one of my voyages across that ocean, and being at length landed, doubtless to their great astonishment and joy, on the American land; but the reader will find the account of this remarkable, and I may say intensely interesting, discovery, with its details, in the continuation of my investigations in Indo-America to verify it and to prove its reality in the sequel.

It was in the year 1833, at the close of the first decade of my colonial life, that I hit upon this great discovery, during my third voyage across the Southern Pacific Ocean to Cape Horn; and in the year 1834 I published in London, with nearly the same title as this volume, a work of upwards of two hundred pages, in which I gave an account of it, as well as of my two previous discoveries, as to the identification of the Malays and Polynesians, and their subsequent history and migrations, and also as to the practicability of crossing the Pacific from the westward.

That volume was published not only to inform the public of the important facts I had discovered, but to prevent the piracy of my discoveries, which I conceived was not at all unlikely, by unscrupulous, or rather unprincipled, persons. That object, however, it did not prevent. For scarcely was my work published when the important discoveries I had effected were first depreciated, and then appropriated wholesale, by persons whom I could never have supposed capable of such iniquity. Having in the meantime returned to the colony myself, I was not aware of the circumstance till the very popular work in which the shameless piracy had been committed was in its sixth thousand. I was then again at sea, on another voyage to England, in the year 1839, when I happened to borrow the book I refer to from the captain of our good ship, who, as an old shipmaster, whaling and trading among the islands, had got a copy of it from a South Sea friend in Sydney. I read the book, I confess, with profound indignation; for by propagating the idea that America was originally discovered and settled from Polynesia, without one syllable of explanation as to how such an idea had originated in my fortunate discovery of 1833, the perpetration of the wrong has in great measure robbed me for forty years past of the credit and the honour of my previous discoveries for ten years in the Pacific Ocean, including, of course, what I consider my great discovery of the way in which the Polynesians had originally crossed over from Easter Island into America. The reader will find the details in the sequel; but, as I had intended from the first to publish a second edition of my book of 1834 at some time or other, with all the additional facts and illustrations I could collect in the meantime in proof of my theory, I have never complained before of the literary piracy through the Press, as I thought I should have a better opportunity of doing so in a second edition.

I could scarcely have been surprised that the evidence adduced to prove the original discovery of America from Polynesia in my very imperfect work of 1834 should have been deemed insufficient and unsatisfactory. But I trust the large additional amount of evidence of all kinds I have adduced in the present volume, in proof of the original discovery and settlement of America by the course and in the way I have indicated from the Pacific, will now be deemed by all candid persons both sufficient and satisfactory. Hundreds of additional proofs of the identity of the Polynesians and the Indo-Americans might easily be collected, if required; but those I have given will, I presume, be sufficient.

During a visit I paid to the United States in the year 1840 I delivered a few lectures on the discovery of America from the Pacific, and as the subject was both novel and attractive, although rather recondite for the American mind, they excited considerable interest, especially in Charleston, in South Carolina, where I had the eminent American ornithologist, Audubon, and a German *litterateur*, who had shortly before been listening to a learned disquisition on the Aztecks in the German university of Freiburg, as my hearers. They were both greatly interested with the whole subject.

I also delivered occasional lectures on the same subject many years since in New South Wales, and in recent years I have repeatedly delivered a series of such lectures before the Royal Society of this colony. But I have never completed my subject till now.

I shall now conclude in the words of the Christian Father, Lactantius, which I would take the liberty to accommodate to the grand question which, I conceive, is now happily solved in this volume—

Omissis ergo hujusce terrenæ philosophiæ authoribus, nihil certi asserentibus, aggrediamur viam rectam.

LACTANTIUS de Falsa Religione, lib. i., c. 1.

Let us, therefore, have done with those uncertain, unsatisfactory and futile attempts of men to people America by Behring's Straits, and let us follow on the right way, which is God's own way, by the Isles of the Southern Pacific Ocean.

# VIEW OF THE ORIGIN AND MIGRATIONS OF THE POLYNESIAN NATION, &c.

## CHAPTER I.

HOW THE POLYNESIAN NATION CAME TO BE SPREAD OVER THE NUMBERLESS ISLANDS OF THE PACIFIC OCEAN.

THE singular phenomenon which the South Sea Islands present to the eye of a philosophical observer is, perhaps, one of the most difficult to account for that has ever exercised the ingenuity of man. From the Sandwich Islands in the Northern, to New Zealand in the Southern Hemisphere; from the Indian Archipelago to Easter Island, adjoining the continent of America—an extent of ocean, comprising sixty degrees of latitude, and a hundred and twenty of longitude (*i. e.*, exactly twice the extent of the ancient Roman Empire in its greatest glory)—the same primitive language is spoken, the same singular customs prevail, the same semi-barbarous nation inhabits the multitude of the isles.

In using this language, however, I would not be understood to include the numerous islands, and groups of islands, of the Western Pacific, the inhabitants of which are all remarkably different from those of the other South Sea Islands, and are evidently derived from the same primitive stock as the aborigines of Australia, and the Papuans of New Guinea. These islanders are all of a much darker hue than those of Polynesia Proper, or the islands to the eastward, many of them being jet black; and there is this remarkable distinction between the two races, that while the languages of Eastern Polynesia are all mere dialects of the same primitive tongue, there is an infinity of languages in the islands of Western Polynesia, and all remarkably different from each other; every island of any size having one of its own, and the larger islands three or four.

Confining our attention, therefore, to the lighter-coloured Polynesian race, and leaving out of view for the present the question as to their original point of departure from the other habitations of mankind, the first question that presents itself for our consideration is by what means, or in what way, has that very remarkable race spread itself over the vast Pacific Ocean—reaching, as they have done, the remotest inhabited islands of both hemispheres, from the Sandwich Islands in the Northern, to New Zealand in the Southern Hemisphere, and stretching across the broadest part of the Pacific in the equatorial regions.

Without condescending, therefore, to notice the theories that have been sometimes advanced on the subject—viz., that the South Sea Islanders are indigenous,† or that their islands are merely the summits of the mountains of a submerged continent or continents that once existed in that part of the terraqueous globe\*—the remarkable

---

† La plupart de ces isles ne sont en effet que des pointes de montagnes; et la mer, qui est au-dela, est une vraie mer Mediterranée.—Buffon. This observation refers to the islands of the West Indies; but it has also been repeatedly made in regard to the numerous groups of Polynesia.

\* Ipsos Germanos indigenas crediderim—quia nec terra olim, sed classibus, advehebantur, qui mutare sedes volebant. Tacit.

phenomenon in the Pacific Ocean being the creation rather than the disappearance of land, in the numberless coral islands that are constantly rising up from the depths of the ocean, and at length becoming solid land—without noticing any further either of these theories, I would observe that the Polynesians, like all other islanders, are a maritime people, very frequently if not constantly at sea, and ever and anon making short voyages from island to island in their respective groups. Now, although the trade-winds that blow from the eastward in both hemispheres are remarkably regular, they are not uniformly so; and in such exceptional cases as do occur, the islanders are occasionally overtaken by storms blowing in a contrary direction to that of the

---

de Morib. German.—" I am inclined to believe the Germans indigenous ; for, in ancient times, those who were desirous of changing their settlements did not usually travel by land, but by sea." By the way, Tacitus would have found no difficulty in peopling the South Sea Islands ; for if their inhabitants had not been allowed to have been *indigenæ*, *i.e.*, to have sprung up out of the sea like the islands themselves, he would have said, *olim classibus advehebantur*, *i.e.*, " they arrived in canoes along time ago."

usual trade-winds, and are carried out perhaps hundreds of miles into the boundless ocean. There are numerous instances on record of this calamitous occurrence having been experienced in the Pacific Ocean; of which I shall mention the few following, for which it will be seen we have the very best authority.

*Schouten* (a Dutch navigator), who traversed the south part of the Pacific Ocean in the year 1615, met with a large double canoe full of people, at about a thousand leagues distance from the Ladrone Islands, towards the south-east.*

In 1696, two canoes, having on board thirty persons of both sexes, were driven by contrary winds and tempestuous weather, on the Island of Samal, one of the Philippines, after being tossed about at sea seventy days, and having performed a voyage from an island called by them Amorsot (otherwise Ancorsa), 300 leagues to the east of Samal. Five of the number who had embarked died of the hardships suffered during this extra-

---

* *Lord Anson's Voyage Round the World*, page 343, London, 1748.

ordinary passage.*

About the time of the commencement of the London Society's Mission (says the Rev. Mr. Ellis), an American seaman, of the name of Robert, accompanied by a number of natives, undertook to convey some books from Rurutu to Rimatara, a distance of about seventy miles. He reached Rimatara in safety; but, on returning, was driven out of his course, and perished with several of his companions. The day after his death the boat was picked up by a vessel, about two hundred miles distant from the island; and by proper treatment, such of the crew as were still alive recovered from the weakness and exhaustion which famine had induced.†

The English missionary from Tahiti was the first foreigner that ever landed on the Island of Rapa; but many years before his arrival, an inhabitant of some other island, the only survivor of the party with whom he sailed from his native shores, had been by tempestuous weather drifted

---

\* *Lettres Edifiantes and Curieuse*, tom xv., p. 196.
† *Polynesian Researches*, vol. III., p. 192.

to the island, and was found there by the native teachers who first went from Tahiti. His name was Mapuagua, and that of his country Manganeva, which he stated was much larger than Rapa, and situated in a south-easterly direction. The people he described as numerous, and much tattooed; the name of one of their gods was the same as that of one formerly worshipped by the Tahitians.*

About twenty persons in number, of both sexes, had embarked on board a canoe, at Otaheite, to cross over to the neighbouring island, Ulietea. A violent contrary wind arising, they could neither reach the latter island, nor get back to the former. Their intended passage being a very short one, their stock of provisions was scanty, and soon exhausted. The hardships they suffered while driven along by the storm, they knew not whither, are not to be conceived. They passed many days without having anything to eat or drink. Their numbers gradually diminished—worn out by famine and fatigue. Four men only

---

* *Polynesian Researches*, vol. III., p. 374.

survived, when the canoe overset, and then the perdition of the small remnant seemed inevitable. However, they kept hanging by the side of their vessel during some of the last days, till Providence brought them in sight of the people of this island, who immediately sent out canoes, took them off their wreck, and brought them ashore. Of the four who were thus saved, one has since died. This Island is called Wateeoo, by the natives. It lies in lat. 20 degrees 1 minute south, and longitude 201 degrees 45 minutes east. It is 200 leagues from the native Island (Otaheite), of the shipwrecked mariners.*

Captain Beechy, R.N., fell in, in the course of one of his voyages in the Pacific, with a party of South Sea Islanders from Tahiti, who had been driven six hundred miles from their native isle, by a gale of westerly wind.

Captain Duke, an old whaling captain, well known in his time in Sydney, with whom I made a voyage to England in the year 1839, told me that he had also fallen in, in one of his whaling

---

\* *Cook's Voyages*, vol. I., page 202 (11th April, 1779).

voyages, with a large canoe filled with South Sea Islanders, with their provisions all but expended, and distant many hundred miles from their native isle. He very kindly took them all on board his ship, and kept them there till he could land them, as he did at length, on their own island.

Another old whaling captain, equally well known in Sydney, in the olden time—I mean Mr. Joseph Thomson, with whom I also made a voyage to England in the year 1824—told me that he had fallen in, in one of his whaling voyages, with a large Tahitian canoe, with a party of natives on board, all but exhausted, and several hundred miles from their native island. He took them on board his vessel and supplied them with all that was requisite for their restoration and refreshment. But, as Tahiti was greatly out of his course at the time, he gave the islanders a compass, and showed them how to steer in order to reach it. The natives, as he afterwards learned, watched their silent guide with intense interest during the whole course of their homeward voyage; and when the summits of the well known mountains of their native isle hove in sight, they leaped up in their canoe and danced for joy. Then looking wistfully first at the land and then at the compass, they said, "The cunning little thing, it saw it all the time."

In the only other case of the kind which I shall mention, and which occurred about thirty-five years since, a whaling captain out of this port, fell in with a canoe drifting about many hundred miles from the nearest land. There were two dead bodies in the canoe, while those who remained alive were in the last stage of exhaustion.

These accidents, arising from sudden squalls have, doubtless, been often aggravated and rendered unnecessarily fatal by the mental character and disposition of the South Sea Islanders themselves; for, conjoining a remarkable proneness to despondency with their spirit of adventure, whenever the wind blows strong and adverse, in their short and frequent voyages from island to island, instead of redoubling their exertions, they generally pull down all sail, and extend themselves in sullen despair along the bottom of their canoes, abandoning themselves and their tiny vessel to the mercy of the wind and waves.

In addition to these cases of accident from squalls and tempests, maritime enterprise, which is the characteristic of islanders, has also led, doubtless in numberless instances, to voyages of discovery on the part of the South Sea Islanders, as Quixotic as that of Columbus must have appeared to most of his contemporaries. For example, a solitary native of the Fiji Islands had been driven to sea by a sudden storm towards the close of last century, when fishing off the shore in his canoe, and had landed at length on the Friendly Islands, 360 miles from his native isle. In such circumstances, no European unacquainted with the science and art of navigation, would have ventured to put to sea in search of the distant island from which the stranger had been accidentally driven. But the thoughtless Polynesian, fired by the spirit of adventure, often disregards the suggestions of prudence in such cases. Stimulated, accordingly, by the intelligence he had thus received from the stranger, of the existence of other islands in a particular direction, Tooi Hata Fatai, a chief of the Friendly Islands, set sail for the Fiji Islands some time afterwards, with two hundred and fifty followers, in three large canoes, each of which must have carried upwards of eighty men, with provisions and water for the voyage. In such voyages, however, the unskilfulness of the pilot, or the unexpected change of the wind, would often carry the adventurous islanders far beyond their reckoning; and in such circumstances they would either founder at sea or perish of hunger, or be driven they knew not whither, till they reached some unknown and previously undiscovered island. In the latter case they would gladly settle on the new-found land, fearful of again trusting themselves to the ocean, and entirely ignorant as to what course they should steer for their native isle. Since the commencement of the present century, and the formation of missionary settlements in certain of the more prominent Polynesian groups, there have been repeated and well authenticated instances of adventurers having left their native islands on such hazardous voyages as the one I have just referred to, and of having never been heard of afterwards.

But the state of society that has hitherto subsisted, from time immemorial, in the South Sea Islands, affords an additional means of accounting for the distribution of man over the vast plain of the Pacific. The South Sea Islands have, in all past time, been, like the ancient Greek democracies, the scene of frequent, if not perpetual, civil war;* and the cruel practice of the victors has generally, if not uniformly, been to exterminate the vanquished, if possible, either by putting them to death as soon as they caught them on land, or by forcing them out to sea.

---

\* During the fifteen years the Rev. Mr. Nott spent in the (Society) Islands, the island of Tahiti was involved in actual war ten different times.—*Polynesian Researches*, I., 275.

At the battle of Hooroto, in which the people of Huahine were engaged with those of Raiatea, the fleet of Huahine consisted of ninety ships, or war-canoes, each about 100 feet long, filled with men.

In this war, the greater part of the chiefs and warriors of the Seaward or Society Islands were destroyed. The island of Huahine never recovered from the effects of this murderous conflict.—*Ibid*, 284, 285.

In the year 1799, when Finow, a Friendly Island chief, acquired the supreme power in that group of islands, after a bloody and calamitous civil war, in which his enemies were completely overpowered, the barbarian forced a number of the vanquished to embark in their canoes and put to sea; and during the revolution that issued in the subversion of paganism in Tahiti, the rebel chiefs threatened to treat the English missionaries and their families in a similar way.

On glancing at the chart of the Pacific Ocean, it would seem probable that the first inhabitants of New Zealand had reached that island from the Friendly Islands, the nearest to New Zealand of all the other Polynesian groups, and distant about nine hundred and fifty miles to the northward. The internal evidence afforded by the dialect of New Zealand confirms this presumption, as it bears a much closer resemblance to that of the Friendly than to that of the more distant Society Islands; while the tradition of the natives is that the first inhabitants of the island arrived from the northward. Supposing, then, that New Zealand had been originally discovered and taken possession of by a party that had sailed, perhaps, on some short voyage, from the island of Tonga, the principal island in the Friendly Islands group, and been accidentally driven to sea, or by a party of vanquished islanders, who had been driven out to sea by their ruthless conquerors, it is evident that, coming from within the Tropics, there would be no word in their language to denote such a substance as *snow*. On seeing the strange substance, therefore, for the first time after their arrival in New Zealand, and ascertaining its coldness and insipidity, it would be quite natural for them to exclaim, when sorrowfully recollecting the comfortable country they had left for ever, " *Tonga diro !* " Tonga lost ! This is the singular phrase in the New Zealand dialect for snow.

In further illustration of the manner in which the South Sea Islands, and especially the solitary and remoter islands have been peopled in the course of ages past, I may state that it has been ascertained that the dialect of the Chatham Islands, situated only a few hundred miles to the eastward of New Zealand, has a much greater resemblance to that of Tahiti or the Society Islands than to that of New Zealand; but that the dialect of Aitutaki, or the Hervey Islands group, and much nearer Tahiti, is identical with that of New Zealand. The only explanation that can be given of these remarkable facts is that some canoe with a party of natives on board had been blown off the coast of Tahiti by some sudden tempest, and had, after a voyage of upwards of a thousand miles, reached the Chatham Islands; and that, in precisely similar circumstances, a canoe with a party of New Zealanders on board had been blown off their own island, and had, after a voyage of perhaps still greater length, been driven upon the remote island of Aitutaki.

Whether the first inhabitants of New Zealand had been driven from their native island by accident, or by the fortune of war, it is impossible to ascertain. There is one singular feature, however, in the political aspect of that portion of the Polynesian nation which I conceive throws some light on the history of their original migration, as well as on the origin of a horrible practice which has certainly been extensively prevalent in that island, as well as in most of the other islands of the Pacific Ocean. The practice I allude to is that of cannibalism; and the feature in the political aspect of the island that serves to account in some measure for the origin and prevalence of that practice in New Zealand, is the absence of everything like a distinction of caste in that group of islands.

The Asiatic distinction of caste, as we shall see presently, has been developed with greater exactness in the Friendly Islands than in most of the other groups. But in the islands of New Zealand, whose first inhabitants were in all likelihood Friendly Islanders, there is no distinction of caste whatever; every New Zealander who is not a prisoner of war, *i.e.* a slave, professing himself a *rangatira*, or gentleman. We cannot suppose, however, that a large canoe filled with natives, either hastily collected after a defeat in time of war, or proceeding on a voyage to some neighbouring island in time of peace—for it must have been by a party of natives in such circumstances that New Zealand was first discovered,—we cannot suppose that such a party of natives should have left the Friendly Islands in which a distinction of caste prevails without having persons on board of various castes. But if the wretched inmates of such a vessel had by any accident been kept so long at sea (as they must necessarily have been ere they reached New Zealand) as to have expended all their stock of provisions, their only and miserable resource (one shudders to think of it) would have been to kill and eat one of their own number. Such a thing, we know, has been done again and again even by Europeans. Now in such a case of direful emergency, the first victim among a party of South Sea Islanders would, doubtless, be the man of lowest caste; for the idea of putting a person of inferior caste on the same level with a noble or chief in any circumstances, would never occur to a Polynesian. It is, therefore, highly probable, from the present state of native society in New

Zealand, that the miserable wretches who first landed on that island had previously been so long at sea, that they had successively killed and eaten every person of inferior caste on board their vessel; and that ere they reached the unknown land, they had become, through absolute necessity, ferocious cannibals. That the taste for human flesh, which had been acquired in this manner by the fathers of the New Zealand nation, should afterwards have been found to minister to the desire of vengeance or been indulged in for its own sake, is not at all extraordinary. We read in the book of Job, chapter xxxi. 31, " Oh that we had of his flesh ! we cannot be satisfied." And in Burckhardt's " Travels in Nubia," we find the fiollowing trait of brutality given as an illustration of the vindictive character of a Nubian tribe—" Among the Hallenga, who draw their origin from Abyssinia, a horrible custom is said to attend the revenge of blood : when the slayer has been seized by the relations of the deceased, a family feast is proclaimed, at which the murderer is brought into the midst of them, bound upon an angareyg (or sofa), and while his throat is slowly cut with a razor the blood is caught in a bowl and handed round among the guests; every one of whom is bound to drink of it at the moment the victim breathes his last."\*

Unknown in Europe, the horrible practice of cannibalism has never obtained in Asia, and is scarcely heard of even in Africa: but its existence and prevalence among the Polynesians was the natural and necessary accompaniment of the discovery and settlement of many of the remotest isles of the vast Pacific Ocean. Cannibalism, in such cases, was the national, the characteristic, the original sin of the race; for it was indispensable to the very existence of the first discoverers of many of the remotest islands that they should have learnt on their passage thither to drink the tepid blood, to devour the quivering sinews, and to gnaw, like a starved hyena, the bones of their fellow-men.

When Shunghee (E Ongi), a New Zealand chief, who had been in England, where he was taken

---

\* Burckhardt's Travels in Nubia, p. 356.

much notice of in certain high quarters in the earlier years of the present century returned to New South Wales, he happened to see Inacki, another chief with whom he had had an ancient feud, in the town of Sydney. He there told his adversary, that when they got back to New Zealand he would fight him. Inacki accepted the challenge; and Shunghee accordingly assembled, on his return to New Zealand, no fewer than two thousand men to attack Inacki. The latter was prepared to receive him, and for some time the event of the battle that ensued was doubtful. At length Shunghee, who had the greatest number of muskets, and who had arranged his men in the form called in Roman tactics the *cuneus* or wedge, placing himself at the apex and directing those behind him to wheel round on the enemy from the right and left, or to fall back into their original position as opportunity offered, shot Inacki. On perceiving his enemy mortally wounded, the savage immediately sprung forward, scooped out the eye of the dying man with his English knife, and instantly swallowed it; and then holding his hands to his throat, into which he had afterwards plunged the knife, and from which the blood flowed copiously, drank as much of the horrid beverage as they could hold. On his return to the Bay of Islands he had about twenty captives bound hand and foot in his war-canoe, whom he intended to retain as slaves. But his daughter, hearing of his arrival, and learning at the same time that her own husband had been killed in the battle, came down to the beach to upbraid her father with being accessory to his death. To pacify her, and to make her some amends for the loss of her husband, Shunghee immediately caused the captives to be laid with their heads over the gunwale of the canoe, and with a sword, which he had received as a present in a high quarter in England, smote off the heads of sixteen of them successively in cold blood.

The heart sickens at such recitals. But these recitals enable us to estimate at what a prodigious expense of human life, and at what a prodigious amount of human suffering, the islands of the South Seas, situated as some of them are at vast distances from the nearest islands, must have been originally peopled. Where one canoe, in the circumstances I have described, was fortunate enough to reach some unknown land in the vast ocean, we may conclude that many must have been lost, after scenes of bloodshed and cannibalism had been transacted on board them, at the very idea of which the imagination revolts with horror. When, however, I find so obvious, so sufficient, and so satisfactory an explanation of the origin and the general prevalence of cannibalism in the South Sea Islands, I feel inclined to be somewhat sceptical in regard to its being a religious observance—bearing a sort of symbolical resemblance, forsooth, to the doctrine of the atonement—as certain *wise men of the east* have supposed. But there are missionaries, as well as philosophers, who are never satisfied with a plain and obvious reason for any thing, if they can only allege one that is either incredible or recondite.

That cannibalism is practised in various islands of the South Seas, where neither necessity nor the desire of vengeance can be urged in palliation of the revolting practice, cannot be doubted. About forty years since, a respectable Scotchman, who had been long in command of a Government vessel out of this port, at a time when it was customary to resort to certain of the South Sea Islands for supplies of pork for the King's stores, told me that when he was lying at the Marquesas, in one of his voyages to these islands, he had seen human viscera hung up for use in the same way as those of a sheep or bullock are frequently seen in England ; and that, on inquiring on one occasion of an elderly woman what had become of a little orphan boy she seemed to be rearing, and to whom he had himself got somewhat attached, he was horrified to learn that the boy had been killed and eaten. Nay, he assured me that he was once offered a human finger himself as a peculiar delicacy.

## CHAPTER II.

FROM WHAT PART OF THE WORLD HAS THE POLYNESIAN NATION ORIGINALLY SPRUNG; AND WITH WHAT PORTION OF THE HUMAN FAMILY DOES IT BEAR THE STRONGEST RELATIONS?

I have no hesitation in expressing my own decided opinion that the Polynesian nation is of Asiatic origin and Malayan race. Before attempting, however, to prove this point, I would observe that there are certain writers who maintain that the Polynesians could not possibly have come from the westward or the continent of Asia, in consequence of the prevalence of the easterly or trade winds of both hemispheres in the Pacific Ocean.

De Zuniga, a Spanish writer of some celebrity and the author of a History of the Philippine Islands, presuming on the uniform prevalence of easterly winds within the tropics, very preposterously combats the idea of the Asiatic origin of the Polynesian nation, and maintains the singular hypothesis that the South Sea Islanders have originally come from the continent of America—crossing the Pacific within the tropics to the islands nearest the American land, and passing successively from island to island till they landed at length on Java, Sumatra, and Madagascar. This amazingly preposterous supposition he endeavours to maintain, moreover, by alleging certain affinities which he conceives subsist between the languages of the Indians of Chili and of the native inhabitants of the Philippine Islands. It is proper, however, to allow the Spaniard to speak for himself.

"Many will urge the absurdity of this supposition, on the plea that the more immediate vicinity of the Philippines to Malacca must have occasioned them to be colonized by the Malays, as our historians generally assert. I do not deny that these islands could easily have been peopled by the Malays; but how could they colonize the Ilas de Palaos and the Marianas, which are distant more than three hundred leagues? And it is still more improbable that they colonized the islands of San Duisk (the Sandwich Islands) and Otaheite, which are distant two thousand leagues from the Philippines. All these people, however, have the same language, the same manners and customs, and consequently the same origin, as our Indians. There is, in my opinion, this other reason for supposing these latter islands could not be peopled from the westward, viz., that in all the torrid zone the east wind generally prevails, which, being in direct opposition to the course from Malacca and the adjacent islands, it is fair to conclude that the inhabitants of all the islands of the South Sea came from the east, sailing before the wind: for we have seen it often happen that the Indians from the Palaos have arrived at the Philippines precisely under these circumstances. On the contrary, we have no instance on record of any of the Philippine Indians having been, even by accident, carried by the winds to the islands to the eastward.* Here, therefore, we appear to have found the most probable solution of our difficulties; that is, that the first settlers came out of the east (we may presume from the coast of South

---

\* This is incorrect, as will be seen from the sequel.

America), and proceeding gradually to the westward, through the Pacific Ocean, *studded as we find it with islands at no very great distance from each other*, and, of course, of easy access before the wind, it follows that to whatever point in an eastern direction we can trace the Tagalic language, we may conclude that at that point emigration must have commenced."*

Preposterous, however, as the theory of De Zuniga may appear to all intelligent and candid persons, we learn, from a work published in London during the present year † that so far from the hypothesis of De Zuniga having been exploded, the Japanese Consul in San Francisco, a Mr. Charles Wolcott Brooks, a gentleman of high character and superior attainments, actually delivered a lecture in advocacy of De Zuniga's theory, before the California Academy of Science in that city, so recently as the 4th of May, 1875.

But the testimony of the illustrious French

---

*" Historia de las Islas Philipinas, por Martinez de Zuniga." i. 2. Manila, 1803.

†" The Native Races of the Pacific States of North America," by Hubert Howe Bancroft, of San Francisco. London, 1876.

navigator, La Perouse, is decisive as to the invalidity of De Zuniga's theory. "Westerly winds," says La Perouse, " are *at least as frequent* as those from the eastward, in the vicinity of the equator, in a zone of seven or eight degrees, north and south; and they, that is the winds in the equatorial regions, are so variable, that it is very little more difficult to make a voyage to the eastward than to the westward."* Again, " It was very clear to me," says Captain (afterwards Admiral) Hunter, the second governor of New South Wales, in the narrative of his voyage from Port Jackson to Batavia, in the year 1791, " from the winds we experienced since we came to the northward of the Line, that at this time of the year, the month of July, and generally during the height of the south-west monsoon in the China seas, these (westerly) winds do sometimes extend far to the eastward of the Philippine Islands, and frequently blow in very heavy gales." At the time he made this observation, Captain Hunter adds, "We were in latitude 13°, 25′ north.

---

\* La Perouse's Voyages, chapter 25.

longitude 121°, 37′ east, Cape Espiritu Santo bearing south 75° west, fifty-eight leagues distant."

In addition to these evidences in favour of the practicability of navigating to the eastward within the equatorial belt of La Perouse, and considerably farther north even, I am happy to be able to appeal to the personal experience of Mr. Edward S. Hill, a well-known and esteemed member of the Royal Society of New South Wales, who, having himself traversed the Pacific Ocean in all directions, but chiefly in the equatorial regions of both hemispheres, for four years of his earlier life, assures me that for three months during the westerly monsoon the prevalent winds in these regions are westerly, while a strong current under their influence sets to the eastward at the rate of two and a half knots an hour.

Besides, with one solitary exception—that of the party of islanders arriving in the Philippine Islands from the eastward, as related in the quotation from the *Lettres Edifiantes et Curieuses*, all the other cases of similar calamitous relations above, were evidently those of vessels driven

far out of their course to the westward by strong,
sudden, and violent westerly gales. It is highly
probable, from the distance traversed, that the
group of islands from which the unfortunate party
had started, in that particular case, must have
been the Marianas or Ladrone Islands. For, if
such a gale as I have supposed had carried the
unfortunate party far to the eastward of these
islands, as soon as it had spent its fury the regular
south-east trade wind would return, and carry
them direct to the Philippines. This idea, which
I cannot but think is a right one, would explain
the extraordinary length of their voyage.

There is, therefore, sufficient reason to believe
that the westerly winds of the Indian Archipelago,
which often blow in heavy gales, having once caught
some unfortunate canoe full of Malays and driven
her upon some unknown island in the Western
Pacific Ocean, where they would have no hope of
ever regaining their native isle; the hapless
islanders and their descendants in succeeding
generations subsequently passed from island to
island to the eastward till they peopled in the

course of ages the numerous equatorial islands of that extensive ocean. And continuing the process from age to age parties of the same maritime and adventurous race, driven from their native isles, whether accidentally or through the fortune of war, were carried in a similar way, as far to the eastward as Easter Island in the south temperate zone, and within about two thousand miles of the American land—as also to the Sandwich Islands in the Northern, and New Zealand in the Southern hemisphere.

Having thus met and disposed of the preliminary objection of De Zuniga and the Japanese Consul of San Francisco, I now proceed to prove my position that the Polynesians are unquestionably of Asiatic origin and Malayan race. I submit, therefore, in the first place, that the distinction of caste, the most ancient and most remarkable feature of Asiatic society, prevails in certain of the more developed groups of the South Sea Islands as fully and formally as in India itself; for in certain other groups it is not observable, for a reason which I have stated above.

I. *Distinction of Caste.*—The King, of course, was supreme; and in Tahiti, or the Society Islands, devotion to royalty was carried to so ridiculous an extent in the case of the royal family, all the members of which were regarded as sacred in the highest Tahitian sense of the word, that whatever any of the princes of the blood happened to touch became sacred also. If the king entered a house the owner had to abandon it forthwith. If he walked on a footpath it was death for a plebeian to walk on it afterwards. In benevolent consideration, therefore, of the welfare and convenience of his subjects, his Tahitian Majesty, having no state carriage, was graciously pleased to be carried on men's shoulders whenever he wished to see the world, lest he should otherwise consecrate his own highways, and render them unavailable in future for his subjects. In certain of the groups of Polynesia, in which there was a regular government established, and the Polynesian system more fully developed, as in the Friendly Islands, the kingly office partook of a dual character, as it still does in Siam, and did till very recently in Japan—there being not only a sort of spiritual sovereign, supposed to be descended from the gods, but a civil and military chief, of the order of nobles, but greatly inferior in rank to the other. But, in the year 1799, when Finow, the dominant chief of the Friendly Islands, had subjected the other chiefs of the group to his authority, he abolished the office of the spiritual chief or Tooi Tonga, as was done a few years ago in Japan, and combining all authority in himself, became like the king the poet speaks of—"Rex Anius,—rex idem, idemque sacerdos." In the Friendly Islands the several castes were well defined; and, as in India the Brahmin, or priestly caste, ranks highest, insomuch that the Grand Lama of these Islands—the Tooi Tonga as he was called—took precedence even of the king.

The castes in India are:—

1. The Brahmin, or priestly caste, whose office is to offer sacrifices, to teach the Veda, to offer gifts, and to receive presents.

2. The Kshutriya, or soldier caste, whose office is to protect the country and the Brahmins.

3. The Vishya, or merchant caste, whose office is to keep cattle, to carry on trade, to cultivate the land.

4. The Shoodra, or servile caste, whose office is to serve the Brahmins. And any persons of the higher castes must not communicate with the lower in marriage, in eating, or in family friendship, on pain of degradation and the loss of all earthly connexions.

In the Friendly Islands, in which the Polynesian system seems to have retained much more of its ancient features than in most of the other groups, a similar, if not the same, division of society obtains. In these islands the highest caste is in like manner :—

1. The priestly caste, the heads of which are supposed to be descended from the gods: they receive presents from the lower castes, and enjoy peculiar privileges; and the other islanders testify their respect towards them by addressing them in a sort of Sanscrit or sacred language, which is not used on inferior subjects.

2. The egi, or nobles, whose office is to preside

in war, and to be the rulers of the country; the king himself being of this caste.

3. The matabooles, or gentlemen, whose office it is to act as companions and counsellors to the nobles, to be masters of ceremonies, and orators at public assemblies. The cadets, or younger brothers and sons of this caste, practise mechanical arts under the name of mooas.

4. The tooas, or lowest caste, consisting of common labourers, cooks, servants; and, in like manner as in India, the repugnance towards any intermingling of the castes is so strong, that if an individual of one of the higher castes has children by a wife or concubine of one of the lower, the children must be put to death to prevent the degradation of the family.

II. The singular institution of *taboo*, which obtains universally in the South Sea Islands, is evidently also of Asiatic origin. The word *taboo* is nearly equivalent to the Latin *sacer* and the Greek *anathema*, signifying either *sacred* or *accursed*, *holy* or *unclean*. Under the Levitical law, the show-bread was *taboo*, or forbidden to all but the priests. The leper was also taboo, for his touch communicated ceremonial pollution. The Jews pronounced the former *holy*—the Romans would have said *Sacer diis cœlestibus* ; the latter they pronounced *unclean*—the Romans would have said *sacer diis infernis*. In short, the Polynesian *taboo* extends to persons, places, and things; and whatever is subjected either to its temporary or to its permanent operation thereby acquires a character of sacredness in the eye of the South Sea Islanders, which it were death to disregard. In New Zealand, for instance, a woman engaged in nursing is *taboo*, and forbidden, under pain of death, to touch the food which she eats with her own hands; and I recollect the case of a woman who had violated this prohibition about fifty years since, by eating a piece of fern root, in the mode forbidden by the law, being killed and eaten.

In some cases, indeed, the *taboo* appears to have been a wise and politic institution. After those national festivals that are so frequent in the South Sea Islands, and at which such vast quantities of provisions are consumed as to threaten a general famine, the *taboo* is laid upon certain articles of food, perhaps for a period of six months, and a supply is thus reserved for the future. In the islands towards the North, certain fruit-bearing trees, and in New Zealand certain plats of *kumara* or sweet potatoes are *tabooed* every season. The produce of these trees or plats is gathered in the time of harvest, and distributed among the people. And in New Zealand, evidently to guard against the events of war and the pressure of famine the seed potatoes are always separated from the rest of the stock at the time of ingathering, and placed in a storehouse which is tabooed; and any person found stealing from such a house is punished with death.

Something analogous to this practice prevailed in ancient times so far to the westward as the territory of Attica; and the circumstance may perhaps induce us to believe, that the superstitions of the ancient Pelasgi had a similar origin with those of the Oriental nations. Throughout the Athenian territory, both on the public lands and on those belonging to private individuals, there were numerous olive trees sacred to the goddess Minerva, of which the fruit was annually collected under the inspection of the magistrates, and afterwards sold by auction; the price being deposited in the public treasury. These trees would have been called taboo by the South Sea Islanders; and the punishment of death, as in the case of the violation of the Polynesian taboo, was awarded by the laws of Athens to the individual who either cut them down or appropriated their fruit. An Athenian citizen, we are told by one of the Grecian historians, was actually tried for his life before the court of Areopagus, for removing the useless stump of one of these trees from his field; and had the fact been proved against him, he would have suffered the sentence of the law.

It may doubtless be difficult to account for so singular an institution as the Polynesian taboo; but its Asiatic origin is evident and indubitable. Its influence and operation may be traced from the Straits of Malacca, across the whole continent of Asia, to the sea of Tiberias and the isles of

Greece. In Ionia, in Hindostan, and in Otaheite, the person, the place, or the thing, that was subjected to the influence of the mysterious taboo, was thenceforth, in the words of the poet, *auguriis patrum et prisca formidine sacrum,*—" abstracted from the common usages of life by a superstitious dread, the result of ancient religious observances." \*

III. Numerous Asiatic customs and observances are practised in the South Sea Islands, as well as in the Indian Archipelago, which closely adjoins the continent of Asia, and must therefore have been originally peopled from it.

To instance only a few of these—in Tahiti, as in Bengal, women are not allowed to eat with their husbands, or to partake of certain articles of food which are indiscriminately eaten by their lords and masters. The general posture in sitting

---

\* During the prevalence of a strict taboo in some of the South Sea Islands not an individual was allowed to move from his place, nor a sound of any kind to be emitted by man or beast. The very pigs had bandages applied to their snouts, and the poultry to their bills, to prevent them from disturbing the solemn stillness of the scene.

is that of the Asiatics—on the ground, cross-legged; and in the Friendly Islands, as in the kingdom of Siam and in other Eastern countries, it is deemed most respectful to sit in the presence of the sovereign. The New Zealanders and Friendly Islanders salute each other by touching noses —a ceremony which is not unknown in Eastern Asia; and in the island of Tonga there is a game called *hico*, which consists in throwing up and keeping in the air a number of balls, as is still practised by the Indian and Chinese jugglers.

Nay, similar modes of thinking, and corresponding peculiarities of action, are found to prevail both in Asia and in the South Sea Islands. The New Zealanders, for example, uniformly ascribe internal maladies to the anger of some atua or divinity, who is supposed to be gnawing the patient's viscera. In such cases, therefore, instead of administering anything in the shape of medicine, the priest or soothsayer is consulted, who, after certain divinations, probably pronounces the patient given over to the anger of the gods, and then tabooes or excommunicates him; after which he is removed to a solitary house in the neighbourhood, and left to die, like the aged or sick Hindoo on the banks of the Ganges; no person being permitted to hold further communication with him, or to supply him with provisions. It is singular, indeed, that a similar idea, and a somewhat similar practice, in regard to the treatment of diseases, should have obtained even among the ancient Greeks. We learn from Homer that when the Grecian army under the walls of Troy was afflicted with an epidemical disease, Machaon and Podalirius, the surgeons-general of the forces, were not asked their opinion in the council of the chiefs, either as to its cause or to the treatment to be adopted for its cure. Chalcas, the soothsayer, was the only person consulted respecting it; and, like a genuine New Zealand ariki, that very sensible person ascribed the disease to the vengeance of the far-darting Apollo.

In the Fiji Islands, the principal wife must be strangled at the husband's death, and buried along with him—a practice evidently borrowed from the suttees of Hindostan. The same practice obtained also in the Friendly Islands, in regard to the principal wife of the Tooi-Tonga, or chief priest of these islands.

It is observed by Mr. Marsden in his History of Sumatra (page 43), " That the original clothing of the Sumatrans is the same with that found by navigators in the South Sea Islands, and in Europe generally, called Otaheitan cloth." And in the account of his voyage from Port Jackson to Batavia, in the year 1791, Captain Hunter observes, in regard to the Duke of York's Island, situated to the eastward of New Ireland, "that most of the natives chew the beetle (betel), and with it used the chenam and a leaf, *as practised in the East Indies*, by which the mouth appeared very red, and their teeth, after a time, became black." " It may be allowed me to remark," says Mr. Marsden, when speaking of the inhabitants of the Pelew Islands, " that these are the most eastern people of whom the practice of chewing *betel* has been mentioned ; nor indeed does it appear that either the nut (*areca*) or the leaf (*piper betel*) is the produce of the South Sea

Islands."* The island, however, in which the practice has been observed by Captain Hunter, the highly-competent observer I have just cited, is situated 20 degrees of longitude, or about 1400 miles to the eastward of the Pelew Islands—a most remarkable and instructive fact, as it shows us, beyond the possibility of doubt, from whence those peculiar customs and observances of the South Sea Islanders, which they practice in common with the inhabitants of Eastern Asia and the Indian Archipelago, have been derived, and how they have travelled to the eastward in ages past.

Captain Hovell, late of the Young Australian, one of the Queensland labour vessels, well known in Sydney, has told me that he had observed the practice of chewing the betel root in Banks' Islands, situated in 170· W. longitude, and in 13· S. latitude, that is considerably farther east than the island mentioned by Admiral Hunter.

The general tradition of the South Sea Islanders, I mean of those inhabiting the groups of the

---

* Marsden's Miscellaneous Works. London, 1834.

Southern Pacific, is that the first inhabitants of the islands came from the northward; Bolotoo, the Paradise of the Friendly Islands, being supposed to be in that direction. In confirmation of this remark, it may be observed that the word *Tonga*, the name of the principal island of that group—signifies *east* both in the Polynesian and Chinese languages; for that designation will doubtless appear peculiarly appropriate as the name of an island which its first discoverers and inhabitants had reached from the westward.

IV. But the evidence afforded by the Polynesian language, in regard to the Asiatic origin of the South Sea Islanders, is still stronger, and less open to objection. "Language," says the celebrated Horne Tooke, "cannot lie; and from the language of every nation we may with certainty collect its origin." "The similitude and derivation of languages," observes Dr. Johnson, "afford the most indubitable proof of the traduction of nations and the genealogy of mankind; they add physical certainty to historical evidence, and often supply the only evidences of ancient emigrations and of the revolutions of ages, which have left no written monuments behind them."

The identity of the languages spoken in the different groups of the South Sea Islands was observed by Captain Cook and his fellow voyagers; and the remarkable resemblance between these languages and those of the Indian Archipelago was also remarked. " In the general character, particular form, and genius of the innumerable languages spoken within the limits of the Indian Islands," observes Mr. Marsden, " there is a remarkable resemblance, while all of them differ widely from those of every other portion of the world. This observation extends to every country, from the north-west extremity of Sumatra to the western shores of New Guinea, and may be even carried to Madagascar on the west, the Philippines to the east, and the remotest of Cook's discoveries to the south."\*

" One original language," observes Sir Stamford Raffles, " seems, in a very remote period, to have

---

\* " Archæologia," vol. vi., page 154.

pervaded the whole (Indian) Archipelago, and to have spread (perhaps with the population) towards Madagascar on one side and the islands in the South Sea on the other: but in the proportion that we find any of these tribes more highly advanced in the arts of civilised life than the others, in nearly the same proportion do we find the language enriched by a corresponding accession of Sanscrit terms, directing us at once to the source whence civilisation flowed towards these regions."\*

"At first," says the unfortunate La Perouse, "we perceived no difference between the language of the people of the Navigators' Islands and that of the people of the Society and Friendly Islands, the vocabularies of which we had with us; but a closer examination taught us that they spoke a dialect of the same tongue. A fact which may tend to prove this, and which confirms the opinion of the English respecting the origin of these people is, that a young Manilese servant,

---

\* History of Java, by Sir Stamford Raffles, p. 369.

who was born in the province of Tagayan, on the north of Manila, *understood and interpreted to us most* of their words. Now it is known that the Tagayan, Talgal, and all the dialects of the Philippine Islands in general, *are derived from the Malay;* and this language, more widely spread than those of the Greeks and Romans were, is common to the numerous tribes that inhabit the islands of the South Sea. To me it appears demonstrated, that these different nations are derived from Malay colonies who conquered these islands at very remote periods; and perhaps even the Chinese and Egyptians, whose antiquity is so much vaunted, are modern compared with these.\*

In confirmation of this idea of the great French navigator, Mr. Marsden informs us that "upon analysing the list of thirty-five Malayan words, of the simplest and most genuine character, twenty will be found to correspond with the Polynesian generally, seven with a small portion of the dialects, and seven, as far as our present knowledge

---

\* La Perouse's Voyages, chap. xxv.

extends, seem to be peculiar to the Malayan itself."*

The following are a few instances, such as Mr. Marsden refers to, of the unmistakable affinity of the Malayan and Polynesian languages:—

| English. | Malay. | Polynesian. |
|---|---|---|
| The eye | Matta (universally) | Mata (universally) |
| To eat | Macan (Javanese Mangan) | Maa (strong guttural, marking the suppression of consonantal sound) |
| To kill | Matté | Matté |
| A bird | Manu (Princes Island Manuck) | Manu |
| Fish | Ika (Javanese Iwa) | Ika |

---

\* As a specimen of the manner in which the dialectic differences of the Polynesian language are developed, take the New Zealand word *Tangata*, signifying man, which, I conceive, is the oldest or original form of the word; in the Tahitian dialect, however, it becomes Taa'ta, with a strong guttural intonation, supplying the omission of the nasal sound. But in the Hawaiian dialect of the Sandwich Islands, in which the letter *k* is substituted for the *t* of the Southern groups, it becomes *kanaka*—a word with which we are rather familiar in these colonies at present, as it is the well-known synonym for what is euphemistically called *labour* by our northern neighbours in Queensland.

| English. | Malay. | Polynesian. |
| --- | --- | --- |
| A louse | Coutou | Outou |
| Water | Vai (Amboynese) | Wai, or Vai |
| The foot | Tapaan | Tapao |
| A mosquito | Gnammuck | Nammou |
| To scratch | Gara | Hearu |
| Coccos roots | Talar | Tara, and Tale |
| A hog | Buai (Achinese) | Buaa |
| Inland | Utan | Uta |
| Name | Ingoa | Ingoa |
| Hair | Ru (Island of Savu) | Huru |
| Fire | Apaui (Achinese) | Auai, obsolete Apauai, Tahitian |
| Man | Orang | Ora (guttural) Tahitian |
| Gentleman |  | Rangatira (New Zealand) |
| Two | Dua | Rua, Dua (New Zealand) |
| Three | Tolu | Toru, Tolu |
| Five | Sima | Dima, Rima (Tahitian) |
| Six | Annam | Ono (New Zealand) |
| Seven | Pitu (Javanese) | Hitu, Witu (New Zealand) |
| Eight | Wolo (Javanese) | Wara, Wadu (New Zealand) |
| Nine | Siwah (Lampong) | Iva |

There is, therefore, abundant reason to believe that the South Sea Islanders, and the various tribes of Malays inhabiting the islands of the Indian Archipelago, are of kindred origin, and that the languages of all these islanders are merely dialects of the same ancient and primitive tongue. The Polynesian branches of that ancient language doubtless bear a closer resemblance to each other than to the dialects of the Indian Archipelago; but this is just what might have been expected, from the comparative isolation of the South Sea Islands on the one hand, and from the vicinity of the Indian Archipelago to the vast continent of Asia on the other.

But before dismissing the item of language, I would observe that there is one remarkable peculiarity in the habitudes of thought among the Indo-Chinese nations, which is also observable among the Malayan and Polynesian tribes, but which, as far as my own knowledge extends, is altogether unknown among the nations—whether Asiatic or European—to the westward of the Ganges. That remarkable peculiarity consists

in their having a language of ceremony or deference distinct from the language of common life. "In addition to these simple pronouns," says Dr. Leyden, in the essay referred to above, "there are various others which indicate rank and situation, as in Malayu, Chinese, and the monosyllabic languages in general, which have all of them paid peculiar attention to the language of ceremony, in addressing superiors, inferiors, and equals." "The distinction of an ordinary language and one of ceremony," observes Mr. Marsden, "exists to a certain degree, among the Malays in practice, although not systematically or compulsorily, as we find it to be the usage among the Javanese."*
"Among the latter," observes Sir Stamford Raffles, in a passage quoted by Mr. Marsden, "nearly one-half of the words in the vernacular language have their corresponding term in the polite language, without a knowledge of which no one dare address a superior." "This distinction," observes Mr. Crawford, in a passage quoted by Mr. Marsden, "by no means implies

---

* Miscellaneous Works, page 21.

a court or polished language, opposed to a vulgar or popular one; for both are equally polite and cultivated, and all depends on the relations in which the speakers stand to each other, as they happen to be inferior or superior. A servant addresses his master in the language of deference, a child his parent, a wife her husband (if there be much disparity in their ages), and the courtier his prince. The superior replies in the ordinary dialect."* But this remarkable peculiarity is equally observable in those of the South Sea Islands, in which there is anything like a regular government or a distinction of ranks. I have already alluded to it in enumerating the various castes into which society is divided in the Friendly Islands; it was also prevalent in Tahiti, and it doubtless affords a strong presumptive evidence of an ancient affinity between the Polynesian and Chinese, or Indo-Chinese nations.

---

* Miscellaneous Works, page 23.

## CHAPTER III.

### AT WHAT PERIOD IN THE HISTORY OF MANKIND DID THE SEPARATION OF THE POLYNESIAN FROM THE MALAYAN NATION TAKE PLACE?

Although there are no historical records to enable us to give a direct answer to this question, there are still certain notes of time recognizable, of which we can avail ourselves, to guide us to a probable conclusion. Oriental scholars, whom I have quoted above, inform us, therefore, that there have been two distinct foreign infusions into the Malayan language; first the Arabic, or comparatively recent, as also the Sanscrit, or ancient infusion. The Arabic infusion was doubtless coeval with the era of Mahomet and the Saracen invasion and conquest of the East. The Sanscrit infusion was of a much earlier date. Now, as there are no Arabic words in the Polynesian language, the separation of the two, on the departure of the first Malayan vessel from some part of the Indian Archipelago into the

Pacific, must have taken place long before the era of Mohamet. But, as there is no Sanscrit element either in that language, the separation of the two nations must necessarily be thrown back to a period of the remotest antiquity.

The modern language of the Malays abounds, therefore, in Arabic words, introduced, along with the Mahometan delusion, by the Moors of the Mogul Empire. It abounds also in Sanscrit vocables—the evidences and remains of the ancient intercourse of the nation with the Hindoos of Western India. The former or more recent of these foreign admixtures, compared with the rest of the language, presents the appearance of a number of quartz pebbles embedded in a sheet of ice--their edges rough and broken, and their general aspect exhibiting nothing in common with the homogeneous mass into which they have been frozen. The result of the latter or more ancient of these admixtures, in consequence of the more liquid character of the Sanscrit language, resembles a compound fluid, homogeneous in appearance, but differing essentially however, from each of the simple ingredients of which it is composed. But the skeleton of the language—its bones and sinews, so to speak—consists of the ancient Malayan or Polynesian tongue. The comparatively consonantal character of the Arabic admixture has introduced into the language a tendency to discard the final vowels of the ancient Polynesian; the polysyllabic character of the Sanscrit infusion has divested it in great measure of its primitive monosyllabic form. But, in getting beyond the influence of these foreign admixtures from the westward, we find the modern language of the Archipelago gradually assimilating to those of Polynesia Proper: for, " in this dialect," observes Mr. Marsden, in reference to the language spoken in the island of Celebes, which is situated at the eastern extremity of the Archipelago, " we observe one feature that assimilates it to the languages of Further Polynesia, the words being invariably made to terminate with a vowel." *

Inattention to these important facts in the history of the Malayan language has led to a series

---

* " Marsden's Miscellaneous Works," p. 46.

of erroneous views on the part of individuals otherwise distinguished for their Oriental scholarship, or for their means of acquiring information on the subject, in their endeavours to ascertain the origin and affinities of the Polynesian language, which have served to involve in still greater obscurity a subject already more than sufficiently obscure. For example, the Rev. Mr. Ellis, the author of that very interesting work, " Polynesian Researches," having embraced the theory of De Zuniga, that the Polynesians are of American origin, has given a list of ten words from Marsden's Malayan Dictionary, the striking dissimilarity of some of which to the corresponding words in the Hawaiian dialect of the Polynesian language induces him to question the identity of the Malayan and Polynesian tongues, although he admits that " there is a striking resemblance in other words," and that " great part of the (Malayan) language was doubtless derived from the same source" as the Polynesian. One of the Malayan words adduced by Mr. E. is the word *shems*, signifying *the sun*, which has certainly no resemblance to the Polynesian word *ra* or *la*. But *shems* is a pure Arabic word, the same as the Hebrew word *shemesh*, and was doubtless never heard of in the Indian Archipelago until after the irruption of the Saracens into India from the west. *Orang*, another of the Malay words adduced by Mr. Ellis, and signifying *man*, has its cognates in the dialects of Otaheite and New Zealand; and so also has the Malay word *macan*, to eat. It will not be thought singular that the Polynesian word *marama* or *malama*, *the moon*, which is actually found in Mr. Ellis's own list of Malayan words in the form of *malam*, should signify *night* in that language; or that the Malayan poetical name for *the sun*, *mata-ari*, *the eye of day*, should not be used in that sense in the Polynesian dialects, in which, however, its component parts exist separately in the words *mata, eye*—and *ao, day*.

Again, that distinguished Orientalist, Sir William Jones, has fallen into a somewhat different mistake in regard to the origin and affinities of the Malayan and Polynesian languages.

Observing that many words in the Malayan language were of Sanscrit origin, and that many words in the dialects of the South Sea Islands coincided with Malayan words of similar sound and signification, Sir William concluded, doubtless rather prematurely, that the Sanscrit of Western India was the common parent of both these eastern tongues. That eminent Orientalist was perhaps overfond of referring everything to the Sanscrit. This ancient mother-tongue was, in his estimation, the key that would open every lock in the labyrinth of language; but it has proved a false key for the equally ancient Polynesian. It was the horse (I will not call it the hobby) on which the great Persian scholar could ride in triumph, like his own Rustan, through all the ancient provinces of Europe—whether Celtic, Teutonic, or Pelasgic—but he was not aware of its inability to force its way through the jungles to the eastward of the Ganges, or to cross over from the continent of Asia to the multitude of the isles.

For that equally eminent Orientalist, Dr. Leyden, whose acquaintance with the languages of Eastern India was much more extensive than that of Sir W. Jones, and whose premature death was one of the greatest calamities that has ever befallen the literature of the East, acknowledges that there are many hundreds, nay thousands, of Sanscrit words in the modern Malayan language,—a circumstance that undoubtedly proves the intimate intercourse that must have subsisted at an early period in the history of the world between the inhabitants of the Archipelago and those of India to the westward of the Ganges,—but distinctly states his conviction that the mass of words in the Malayan language is not derivable from the Sanscrit.\*

In endeavouring, however, to account for the origin and affinities of the dialects of the Indian Archipelago and of Polynesia, Dr. Leyden, in a most interesting essay "On the Languages and Literature of the Indo-Chinese nations," published in the 10th volume of the "Asiatic Researches," and after him Mr. Crawfurd, in his

---

\* On the Languages and Literature of the Indo-Chinese Nation, a Paper by Dr. Leyden, in the 10th volume of the "Asiatic Researches."

"History of the Indian Archipelago," have advanced an hypothesis which has been very judiciously controverted by Mr. Marsden, and which is equally gratuitous and unnecessary. Forgetful of the axiom,

> Nec Deus intersit, nisi dignus vindice nodus,
> Inciderit,

these gentlemen have supposed that there must have been some general language more ancient and more widely diffused than either the Polynesian, the Malayan, or any of the other dialects of the isles; and that these dialects are merely the modifications of that more ancient language, produced by conquest and immigration, just as the French, the Italian, and the Spanish, are the modifications of the Latin or Roman language— the ancient general language of Europe. In short, there is no reason whatever for supposing that the Polynesian, the Malayan, and the other insular dialects, have any such relationship to a common mother-tongue. These dialects are themselves the mother-tongue, or rather its genuine representatives; and Mr. Marsden, therefore, very properly asks, " What evidence is there of any language having been used by this race of people antecedently to that which now so widely prevails?"*

The voice of history informs us that at a period of time very shortly posterior to the deluge, the eastern parts of Asia towards the Yellow Sea were occupied by a people comparatively civilised. " Chinese authors," says the Jesuit Du Halde, in his History of China, " consider *Fo hi* as the founder of their monarchy, who, about two hundred years after the deluge, reigned at first in the confines of the province of *Chen si*, and afterwards in the province of *Ho nan*, which is situated almost in the heart of the empire, where he employed himself in clearing all that tract of land that extends to the eastern ocean. However, this is certain, that China was inhabited above 2155 years before the birth of Christ, which is demonstrable by an eclipse that happened that year, as may be seen in the Astronomical Observations

---

\* " Marsden's Miscellaneous Works," page 13.

extracted from the Chinese history and other books in that language, and published in 1729."*

And there is reason to believe, that at a period not less ancient, or at least shortly thereafter, the foundations of the Malayan state were laid, in the regions to the southward, and in the isles of the Indian Archipelago, by a people acknowledging the same parentage, and speaking the same primitive tongue. Centuries before the Portuguese ensign had been unfurled in the east, the ancient Malayan empire in the island of Sumatra had declined and fallen; the tributary Rajahs had made themselves independent; and the state of Achin, which was governed by one of their number, had become a first-rate maritime power. But there were other powerful maritime states, at the same period, of Malayan origin in the east; and the last fitful struggles of these states with the overwhelming power of Europeans were not unworthy of a people who had maintained without a rival from time immemorial the empire of the eastern seas.

---

* Du Halde, vol. ii., page 2.

A glance at the Malayan empire in the east— not indeed in the period of its rise and progress and vigorous existence, (for history affords us no information on that subject), but in the state it first exhibited to Europeans, that of its decline and fall, may not be uninteresting in this stage of our progress, in showing us what sort of people they were from whom the forefathers of the Polynesian nation originally sprung. It is generally allowed that the islands of Java and Sumatra were the earliest settled by the Malayan nation: these fertile islands may therefore be considered as the head-quarters and the nurseries of their race. There the Malays founded, at an early period, the flourishing and powerful kingdoms of Menangkabau, Acheen, Majapahit, and Japara: the second and the last of which were still so formidable from their maritime force, at a comparatively recent period, as to have almost annihilated the Portuguese empire in the east. Of the first of these ancient kingdoms, Mr. Marsden, who was for some time resident in the island of Sumatra, of which he has given a very interesting account, relates the following particulars:—

"In ancient times the empire of Menangkabau, whose capital of the same name is situated in the interior of Sumatra, on the equinoctial line, seems to have comprehended the whole of that large island; the independent chiefs or rajahs, who have seized upon its divided members and assumed sovereign authority along the coast, still acknowledging the claims of the royal family of Menangkabau as the lords paramount of the island, and still giving them nominal deference. From their possession of a written language, and the general diffusion of the knowledge of reading and writing throughout the island, as well as from the state of the arts, which at present seem to have declined from their former condition, it would seem that in former times this empire had been much more advanced in civilization than it is at present. One of the great districts into which the island was anciently divided, was denominated Malayo, and its inhabitants *orang Malayo*, or Malays—a name which has since become synonymous with *orang Menangkabau,* or Sumatran Mahometan; the other inhabitants of the island being, for the most part, idolators. The district so denominated is situated in the south-eastern extremity of Sumatra, on the river Malayo, which flows into the river of Palembang. About the year 1160, the people of this district emigrated under their rajah, Sri Turi Briwana, to the south-eastern extremity of the opposite peninsula; and, from their settlement there, the peninsula came to be distinguished by the name of *Tanah Malayo,* or Malayan land.

" On this coast the Malays built their first city, Singapura, where they were much harassed for a long time by the kings of Majapahit, a flourishing and powerful state in the neighbouring island of Java. In consequence of this annoyance, the Malayan rajah retired to the western coast of the peninsula, and built the city of Malacca, so called from a fruit-bearing tree of that name which abounds in its vicinity, in the year 1252. In this new settlement the Malays increased rapidly both in numbers and importance, and successfully resisted repeated attacks from the king of Siam, who, in the fourteenth and fifteenth centuries, had become jealous of their power. In 1511 Malacca was taken by the Portuguese, in the reign of Sultan Mahmud Shah, the twelfth king of the Malays, and the seventh of Malacca. In confirmation of these statements, the Malays of the peninsula uniformly assert that they all came from Sumatra."

The state of the art of navigation among the Malayan nations of the Indian Archipelago in former times may be inferred from the following facts. Shortly after the establishment of the Portuguese in Malacca, in the year 1511, the king of Acheen, a state of very considerable power in the north of Sumatra, waged a long and bloody war against them. In the course of this war " Francesco de Mello being sent in an armed vessel, in the year 1527, from Malacca, with despatches to Goa, met near Acheen Head with a ship of that nation just arrived from Mecca, and supposed to be richly laden. As she had on board three hundred Achinese and forty Arabs, he dared not venture to board her, but battered her at a distance, when suddenly she filled and sank, to the extreme disappointment of the Portuguese, who thereby lost their prize; but they wreaked their vengeance on the unfortunate crew, as they endeavoured to save themselves by swimming, and boasted that they did not suffer a man to escape."*

"In the year 1573, after forming an alliance with the queen of Japara, the object of which was the destruction of the European power, the king of Acheen appeared again before Malacca with ninety vessels, twenty-five of them large galleys, with seven thousand men, and great store of artillery. In the year following Malacca was invested with an armada from the queen of Japara of three hundred sail, eighty of which were junks of four hundred tons burden. After besieging the place for three months, till the very air became corrupted by their stay, the fleet retired with little more than five thousand men of fifteen thousand that embarked on the expedition.

" Scarcely was the Javanese force departed,

---

* Marsden's "Hist. of Sumatra," p. 423-424.

when the king of Acheen once more appeared with a fleet that is described as covering the Straits. He ordered an attack upon three Portuguese frigates that were in the road protecting some provision-vessels; which was executed with such a furious discharge of artillery, that they were presently destroyed with all their crews."\*

" In 1582, the king appeared again before Malacca with a fleet of a hundred and fifty sail, and a few years afterwards with three hundred sail. In 1615, he again attacked the settlement with a fleet of five hundred sail and sixty thousand men."†

It would thus appear that on the first opening of the East to Europeans, there were extensive, powerful, and flourishing maritime states of ancient standing established in the Indian Archipelago; the enterprising and warlike population of which had made no inconsiderable progress in the arts of civilization. The conquests of the Arabs, and the voyages of their seafaring converts

---

\* Marsden's "Hist. of Sumatra," p. 431.
† Marsden, *passim*.

in the east to the sepulchre of the Arabian prophet, may, doubtless, account for the prevalence of the Malayan language in the island of Madagascar, although it is much more probable that the settlement of that island had been effected long anterior to the era of Mahomet or the rise of the Saracen power; but the early discovery and the successive settlement of all the islands of the Indian Archipelago were the natural and the necessary result of the existence of an ancient maritime power in that galaxy of isles. Some of these discoveries were, doubtless, the result of accident; others the reward of enterprise. With the islands more favourably situated, a precarious communication would doubtless be maintained for a longer period with the mother country; but as the discovery and settlement of the more distant and isolated isles would in all likelihood be effected by the crews of vessels that had lost their way on the deep sea, their future inhabitants would necessarily remain completely isolated from the rest of mankind.

There is still another and unexceptionable means of ascertaining the period at which the forefathers of the Polynesian nation were finally separated from the rest of mankind, in one or other of the ways I have indicated above. I mean from the character and style of their architectural remains. From the Pyramids of Egypt and the other enormous remains of antiquity in that country, it is evident that the character and style of its architecture, at least for all public or national buildings, was pyramidal and colossal.*
Now it appears to me that that style of the earlier postdiluvian architecture must have been derived from the reminiscences of the antediluvian period, by those eight persons who survived the deluge, and who, we know, were unquestionably not barbarians, but in a comparatively advanced state of civilization. For, as emigrants from the old

---

\* As the Roman poet says of his countrymen in their best days—
"Privatus illis census erat brevis;
Commune magnum."
Which I may be permitted to translate:—Their private buildings were comparatively humble, their public magnificent; so it seems to have been with the ancient Egyptians.

world to any colonial field beyond seas uniformly reproduce, in their new settlements, the whole framework of society as it exists in their fatherland, and in particular its style and character of building, so would the survivors of the deluge reproduce in the world after the flood the whole framework of society, and especially the style of buildings among the antediluvians.* And in a state of things in which the term of human life extended to nearly a thousand years, it was natural that its architecture, for public buildings at all events, should be of a gigantic and colossal character; as time, on the one hand, would be no object to the antediluvian architect, while it would be absolutely necessary, on the other, that buildings, designed to last for generations, should be of such a character as to endure for ages. At all

---

* The original colonists of Rio de Janeiro, in the Brazils, had emigrated from the city of Oporto in Portugal, and those of the Cape of Good Hope from Rotterdam and the other cities of Holland. In both cases the mother-country is strongly reproduced in the style of their buildings. And it has often been observed that the English colonists uniformly build after the pattern of the old country, however unsuitably for the climate.

events, it is unquestionable that the character and style of the architecture prevalent in the world when the forefathers of the Polynesian nation came to be separated from the rest of mankind must have been of the earlier postdiluvian character. For, strange and unaccountable as it may seem, it is nevertheless the fact that the style and character of the architecture for all public buildings throughout the Pacific is pyramidal and colossal. But as I shall have a fitter opportunity in the sequel for referring to this very remarkable fact, I shall merely mention it for the present as a satisfactory proof of the great antiquity of the Polynesian race.

## CHAPTER IV.

WHAT COURSE THE FOREFATHERS OF THE POLYNESIAN NATION MUST, IN ALL LIKELIHOOD, HAVE TAKEN IN THEIR VOYAGES TO THE EASTWARD ACROSS THE PACIFIC OCEAN.

ALTHOUGH I had felt confident, from a comparatively early period, that the forefathers of the Polynesian nation must have started on their easterly migration across the Pacific Ocean from the Indian Archipelago; I was long uncertain, chiefly from my inacquaintance at the time with the course of the winds and currents of the Pacific, as to what particular part of the Archipelago could be fixed on with any degree of probability as their point of departure. But from the information I have since obtained, in addition to my own experience and observation on these subjects, from my Australian friend, Edward S. Hill, Esq., I have been led to conclude with that gentleman that the original starting point of the Polynesians from the Indian Archipelago was the Philippine Islands. A sudden and violent westerly gale, such as often occurs in these regions during the westerly monsoon, in the months of January, February, and March, may have seized some unfortunate Malayan vessel when passing from island to island among the Philippines, and carried her out so far to sea in an easterly direction as to preclude the possibility of her ever regaining the native isle of her crew. In such circumstances they would gladly settle on the first habitable land to which the adverse gale had driven them, in the Western Pacific, and thus give their first inhabitants to the multitude of the isles.

There are two groups of Islands in the Western Pacific, to either of which a vessel caught suddenly by a north-westerly gale off the east coast of the Philippines might be driven, viz., the Palaos or Pelew Islands, in latitude 7° 30' N., and the Marian or Ladrone Islands, in latitude 19° N.; the former of these groups being five hundred and twenty-five and the latter from a thousand to twelve hundred miles from the Philippines. The ship Antelope, Captain Wilson, of the late Hon.

East India Company's service, having been wrecked on the Pelew Islands, in the year 1782, an interesting account of them was afterwards published by Captain Wilson, in which we recognise in the natives of these islands, and especially in the style of their buildings, a people of the regular Polynesian type. The Island of Tinian, of the other or Marian group, was visited and described by Lord Anson in his famous voyage round the world in the years 1740-4; and it is worthy of remark that in that island we find numerous colossal remains of a hoary antiquity, such as are found scattered over the whole face of the Pacific, often even in the smallest islands. The following is an extract from Lord Anson's description of this island, which we may doubtless regard as the first stage in the progress of the Polynesian race from their point of departure in the Philippines to the Far East. The island is twelve miles by six, and is situated in latitude 15° 28' N. It is a beautiful island, and wonderfully fertile.

"There are, in all parts of the island, a great number of ruins of a very particular kind. They usually consist of two rows of square pyramidal pillars, each pillar being about six feet from the next, and the distance between the rows being about twelve feet. The pillars themselves are about five feet square at the base, and about thirteen feet high, and on the top of each of them there is a semi-globe, with the flat part upwards. The whole of the pillars and semi-globes are solid, being composed of sand and stone cemented together and plaistered over."*

Taking it for granted, therefore, that the point of departure for the forefathers of the Polynesian nation from the Indian Archipelago was the Philippine Islands, Mr. Hill—to whose opinions on such subjects I attach the highest value, as being the result of long personal experience and highly-discriminating observation†—supposes that their

---

\* A Voyage Round the World, in the years 1740-4, by George Anson, Esq., Commander-in-Chief of a Squadron of His Majesty's ships, sent upon an Expedition to the South Seas. London, 1748. Page 312.

† Mr. Hill spent four years of his earlier life in traversing the inter-tropical regions of the Pacific Ocean in both hemispheres.

further progress to the eastward was along the chain of the Caroline Islands, which extends in latitude 7° 30' N., the latitude of the Pelew Islands, twenty degrees of longitude, or twelve hundred miles due east. During their progress in this direction they would have both a westerly wind and a strong easterly current during the westerly monsoon months, and they would probably leave part of their number from time to time, as they had evidently done at Tinian, to occupy and settle the more eligible islands on their way. From the eastern extremity of the Caroline chain, the distance eastward to the Radack Islands, the next point of occupation, is four hundred miles.

It is, of course, to be understood that, as the Polynesians had no compass or chart to guide them in their migrations, the discovery and settlement of each successive island or group of islands would be purely accidental: from their being driven off unexpectedly from their proper course by foul winds, if not from the fortune of war or the spirit of adventure, and left either to find some previously unknown island or to perish in the waters. Now as there would doubtless be different, independent, and simultaneous streams of emigration, in different directions and in both hemispheres, in the progress of the discovery and settlement of the numerous islands and groups of islands in the Pacific, Mr. Hill suggests the following as being the probable lines of movement, with the distances in each case.*

From the Radack Islands, as a centre of movement, to the Hawaiian or Sandwich Islands, which there is reason to believe were an early or primitive discovery, the distance is 1900 miles. But, supposing that the Fanning, Washington, Palmyra, and Christmas Islands, to the eastward, had been previously discovered, the distance from thence to Hawaii would be only 1200 miles.

From the Sandwich Islands to the Marquesas, which must also have been a very ancient discovery, the distance is 1800 miles; but from Fan-

---

* Any person desirous of verifying or testing Mr. Hill's suggestions, can easily do so for himself by glancing at a map of the Pacific Ocean.

ning's Island and the Washington group it is only 1200 miles.

From the Marquesas to the Powmotoo Islands, the distance is 350 miles, and from these islands to Tahiti, 350 also.

From thence (that is, from Tahiti), observes Mr. Hill, there is a continuous range of islands towards Easter Island, the farthest east of Captain Cook's discoveries in the Pacific; the last island in the range being distant from Easter Island 800 miles.

Mr. Hill is of opinion that, after reaching Tahiti, Polynesian emigration took a westerly direction to Aitutaki or the Hervey group, distant 500 miles; thence to the Navigators' Islands 700 miles; and thence by a continuous chain to Tonga or the Friendly Islands. The distance from Tonga, to which tradition points as its mother country, to New Zealand, is 950 miles.

Simultaneously with the emigration to the southward, Mr. Hill supposes that there must have been a north-westerly emigration from Tonga, or the Friendly Islands, to Wallis and Horne Islands, distant 350 miles; thence, running with the south-east trades, by Mitchell, Ellice, and Depeyster islands up to the Kingsmills group, the northern parts of which are within 300 miles of the Radack and Rollick chain. From the Sandwich Islands and the Marquesas, the language is identical throughout this route to the Kingsmills. There the line of continuity in language ends—the Papuan or Western Polynesians having for their eastern limit the Fiji Islands.

Such, then, in all probability, is the manner in which the multitude of the isles of the vast Pacific Ocean have been progressively discovered and settled during the past four thousand years; for I cannot, for the reasons I have stated above, assign a shorter period for the process. And considering the very imperfect means of navigation possessed by the Polynesian race, and their previous entire ignorance of the vast ocean on which their lot was originally cast, one cannot think without horror of the scenes of bloodshed and cannibalism that must have been enacted on that vast ocean before this wonderful result could have been achieved.

Perhaps the most remarkable feature of Polynesian life is the aspect with which we are everywhere presented in the South Sea Islands of an ancient but extinct civilization. If the people are barbarians now, it is abundantly evident that they were not always so, but that they are the descendants of a race of men who were once in a comparatively high state of civilization. The monuments of that civilization are to be found all over the Pacific, and there is no possibility of alleging, as is done in another case of a similar kind, to which I shall have to refer in the sequel, that these monuments of ancient but extinct civilization were the productions of a different race from that which now inhabits these islands; for there is no probability of any other race than the present having ever existed in the South Seas.

The Malays, from time immemorial, have always been a maritime people, and there are not wanting evidences of superior skill in maritime affairs even among the Polynesians of the present day. In the Gilbert Islands, on the Equator, they still construct vessels—immense canoes, raised upon and decked, and having their planks bound together with sinnet or the cordage made from the husks of the cocoanut—capable of holding 150 men. Nay, these islanders can not only make voyages of considerable length in such vessels, but can pilot themselves and steer their course by the stars. And while in some islands the natives cannot count more than five, these islanders can reckon up thousands with perfect facility. In the Island of Tonga, one of the Friendly Islands, there is an ancient monument called the Tomb of Toobo-Tooi, consisting of immense blocks of stone, which the present inhabitants of the island are quite unable to move. But these blocks must not only have been moved and fixed in their places, but rafted across the sea in such vessels for the purpose as I have just described, as there is no stone of the kind to be found in Tonga; the island being of coral formation and perfectly level, and without a stone of any kind larger than a pigeon's egg. All this implies such a degree of architectural skill and mechanical power as the present inhabitants can only conceive of as having been the work of the atuas or gods.

There is also abundant evidence in the South Sea Islands of these islands generally having at one time been inhabited by a much larger population than there is now; and in some cases—as in Fanning's Island, when first discovered by Europeans—there were no inhabitants on the island at all, although there was abundant evidence of its having been at some past time inhabited by a people of Polynesian race. Whether the inhabitants had all been cut off by some epidemic, or had put off to sea in a body in search of some happier isle, can never of course be known. But there are peculiar sources of depopulation in the South Sea Islands, of which internecine war and infanticide are doubtless the chief. One can have no idea, from the war practices of European nations, of the frightful character and atrocities of wars in the South Sea Islands. I once visited a Golgotha, or place of skulls, at some distance from the town of Auckland, in the Northern Island of New Zealand. The natives of the place having a mortal feud with a tribe in the Bay of Islands, the latter took the unusual course of making a long journey by night;

and finding their enemies asleep, massacred the whole tribe, with the exception of a girl who escaped—the whole affair being succeeded by a cannibal feast on the bodies of the dead.*

But there is a practice in Polynesian warfare perhaps still more atrocious. The word *Tiputa* in the Tahitian language signifies what the Spaniards call a *poncho*, being a square mat with a hole in the centre, through which the head is thrust; the mat falling down gracefully both before and behind. Now, the practice I allude to among the Tahitian braves was, for the warrior who had slain his enemy in battle to stretch his dead body on the ground, and after scooping out the viscera, to make a hole through the back, large enough to

---

* The total extermination of their enemies, and the utter desolation of their country, was often the avowed object of the native wars. And this design, horrid as it is, has often been literally accomplished. Every inhabitant of the hostile island, with the exception of the few who had perhaps escaped by flight in their canoes, has again and again been massacred. The bread-fruit trees, the principal source of subsistence for the inhabitants, have been cut down and left to rot; the cocoa-nut trees have been killed by cutting off the tops or crown, leaving the stems in desolate leafless ranks, as if they had been struck by lightning.—" Polynesian Researches," I., 293.

admit his head, with a stone hatchet. The horrible garment being thus prepared, the savage thrusts his head through the hole in the dead man's body, so arranging the dead body that the head and arms should hang down in front, and the trunk and limbs behind. In this horrific guise the savage marched in triumph among his friends. Nay, the practice was so common among the bloodthirsty savages that they had actually a particular name for it, viz.—*Tiputa-Taata,* or *Man-poncho.*

Infanticide, or child-murder, has also been a fruitful source of depopulation among the more advanced groups of the South Sea Islands. The Areoi Society of Tahiti—an infamous association, the principle of which was to murder all the offspring of its members—contributed greatly during the prevalence of heathenism in the islands towards this lamentable issue; and since the conversion of the Society Islands to Christianity, there have been many distressing cases of parents who had murdered their children under the reign of heathenism stating the fact, and expressing their sincere repentance and deep regret at public meetings held in the islands. The following is a very interesting case of the kind:—

"At a public meeting held in the Island of Raiatea, one of the Society Islands, and the one which is regarded by the native tradition as the first settled of the group, a venerable chief rose, and addressed the assembly with impulsive action and strongly excited feeling. Comparing the past with the (then) present state of the people, he said " I was a mighty chief—the spot on which we are now assembled was by me made sacred for myself and family: large was my family, but I alone remain—all have died in the service of Satan—they knew not this Good Word which I am spared to see; my heart is longing for them, and often says, within me, 'Oh, that they had not died so soon.' Great are my crimes; I am the father of nineteen children—*all of them I have murdered*—now my heart beats for them. Had they been spared they would have been men and women, learning and knowing the Word of the true God; but, while I was thus destroying them, no one, not even my own cousin (pointing to Tamatoa, the King, who presided at the meeting) stayed my hand, or said 'spare them.' No one said the good Word, the true Word, is coming, spare your children ; and now my heart is repenting, is weeping for them."*

Independently, however, of all assignable causes, it would seem to be a mysterious arrangement of Divine Providence that the inferior races of mankind, with the exception, perhaps, of the African negro, should die out when they come in contact with Europeans. Not only the civilization, but the vital principle of the nation seems to become gradually feebler and feebler till, at length, it becomes extinct. This is evidently the process now in rapid progress, notwithstanding every effort to counteract it, among the Polynesian tribes from the Sandwich Islands in the North to New Zealand in the South.

To sum up the argument of this chapter, Mr. Hill's opinion, in which I entirely concur, is that the forefathers of the Polynesian nation, with

---

* Polynesian Researches, II., 329.

their descendants, perhaps for many successive generations, crossed the Pacific to their farthest east, in the Northern Hemisphere; and that, afterwards crossing the Line, their emigration thenceforth took, successively, a westerly, southerly, and north-westerly direction.

I infer, moreover, from the lights of the past, that the persons who effected these extensive emigrations were not barbarians, but in a comparatively high state of civilization, and that they brought with them, to the farthest east, their maritime skill, and their extraordinary knowledge and control of the mechanical powers. Look at Easter Island, the farthest east of the Polynesian race, and say whether the colossal remains of a hoary antiquity, which Captain Cook and his fellow-voyagers found there, could have been the workmanship of a barbarous people?

The following is Captain Cook's account of his visit to Easter Island, in March, 1774, upwards of a hundred years since. The island, I may observe, is in latitude 27° 6', and is only ten or twelve leagues in circuit. It has no harbour of any value to maritime powers of the present day, and yet how populous it must have been in those days of a hoary antiquity, of which it presents us with such remarkable remains.

Easter Island, visited by Captain Cook, March, 1774.

"On the east side, near the sea, they met with three platforms of stone-work, or rather the ruins of them. On each had stood four of those large statues; but they were all fallen down from two of them, and also one from the third; all except one were broken by the fall, or in some measure defaced. Mr. Wales measured this one, and found it to be fifteen feet in length, and six feet broad over the shoulders. Each statue had on its head a large cylindric stone of a red colour, wrought perfectly round. The one they measured, which was not by far the largest, was fifty-two inches high, and sixty-six in diameter. In some the upper corner of the cylinder was taken off, in a sort of concave quarter-round, but in others the cylinder was entire.

"They observed that this side of the island was

full of those gigantic statues so often mentioned; some placed in groups on platforms of masonry; others single, fixed only in the earth, and that not deep; and these latter are in general much larger than the others. Having measured one which had fallen down, they found it near twenty-seven feet long, and upwards of eight feet over the breast and shoulders; and yet this appeared considerably short of the size of one they saw standing; its shade, a little past two o'clock, being sufficient to shelter all the party, consisting of near thirty persons, from the rays of the sun.

"The gigantic statues so often mentioned, are not, in my opinion, looked upon as idols by the present inhabitants. On the contrary, I rather suppose that they are burying places for certain tribes or families. I, as well as some others, saw a human skeleton lying on one of the platforms, just covered with stones. Some of these platforms of masonry are thirty or forty feet long, twelve or sixteen broad, and from three to twelve in height, which last in some measure depends on the nature of the ground, for they are generally at the brink of the bank facing the sea, so that their face may be ten or twelve feet, or more, high, and the other may not be above three or four. They are built, or rather faced, with hewn stones of a very large size, and the workmanship is not inferior to the best masonry we have in England. They use no sort of cement, yet the joints are exceedingly close, and the stones morticed and tenanted one into another in a very artful manner. The side walls are not perpendicular, but inclining a little inwards, in the same manner that breastworks, &c., are built in Europe; yet had not all this care, pains, and sagacity been able to preserve these curious structures from the ravages of all-devouring time.

"The statues, or at least many of them, are erected on these platforms, which serve as foundations. They are, as near as we could judge, about half length, ending in a sort of stump at the bottom, on which they stand. The workmanship is rude, but not bad, nor are the features of the face ill-formed, the nose and chin in particular; but the ears are long beyond proportion, and, as to the bodies, there is scarcely anything like a human figure about them.

"We could hardly conceive how these islanders, wholly unacquainted with any mechanical power, could raise such stupendous figures, and afterwards place the large cylindrical stones, before mentioned, upon their heads."*

When Commander Powell, of H.M.S. Topaze, visited Easter Island, in the year 1868, and carried home one of the colossal statues, or idols, for the British Museum, there were not fewer than thirty-six of these statues on the highest ridge of the island. The one Captain Powell carried home actually weighed five tons, and the average weight of the others was from one to five tons. The natives demurred, at first, to the removal of the statue; but, when the object of doing so was explained to them, so far from throwing any obstacle in the way, they even assisted in rolling down the statue from the heights to the shipping.

---

*" Captain Cook's Voyages," vol. III., page 288. London: 1821.

## CHAPTER V.

The Westerly Winds that had Propelled the Forefathers of the Polynesian Nation, from their Original Starting Point in the Philippine Islands, to their farthest East, in Easter Island — a Distance of upwards of Seven Thousand Miles, across the broadest part of the Pacific Ocean — must have Carried them across the remaining Narrow Tract of Ocean to the American Land, and given its first Inhabitants to America.

It is evident, from the cases recorded in the first chapter of this work, that westerly winds were generally foul winds in the Western Pacific: the trade winds of both hemispheres being east winds. They were therefore unexpected, sudden, and violent; and they often caught the unfortunate canoe when a short way off the land for any purpose, and carried its crew hopelessly and for ever away to the eastward, either to find some previously unknown island in that direction, or to perish in the waters.

It is equally evident that the easterly migrations of the Polynesian nation must all have occurred during the existence of that ancient and long-extinct civilization of which we have just been observing the colossal remains in Easter Island. The people who constructed those terraces, or platforms, and erected those statues we have been contemplating in that island, were not barbarians, but people in a comparatively high state of civilization. But that civilization would certainly not have ensured them against one at least of the peculiar perils of Polynesian life in all past ages, their being caught in a sudden and violent westerly gale and carried far beyond reckoning to the eastward. One of these accidents that have been occurring in Polynesia for all time past, may therefore have occurred in the case of some unfortunate native vessel off Easter Island, and carried her across the intervening tract of ocean to the continent of America.

I had been led to this idea by the information

bearing on the subject which I had gained from my own personal experience in regard to the winds of the Southern Pacific Ocean; for on a voyage to England by Cape Horn, in the year 1830, we had, after doubling the North-East Cape of New Zealand, encountered a violent south-east gale of seven days; the wind right ahead, and the mountains of New Zealand in sight far to the westward. When this adverse gale had spent its fury, it was succeeded, to our great joy, almost instantaneously by a strong westerly gale, which carried us, with close-reefed topsails, and without intermission, at the rate of ten or eleven knots an hour, right across the Pacific to Cape Horn. Now, if such a westerly gale as I had thus experienced myself would extend considerably to the northward of Easter Island,* it was perfectly warrantable to suppose that if there had occurred one of those accidents that have been of constant occurrence in the Pacific from time immemorial—that of a

---

\* Mr. Hill, in his paper, *penes me*, thus writes:—" In winter the west winds south of the Equator frequently extend north of the latitude of Easter Island."

large canoe or other coasting vessel, such as would be used by the natives of Easter Island during the period of their ancient but long-extinct civilization, being caught off that Island in such a westerly gale as I have described, she would be carried without fail across the intervening tract of ocean to the American land. In short, my theory, or rather my firm belief and conviction, is, that the American continent was originally discovered by a party of famished Polynesians who had been caught suddenly in a violent gale of westerly wind off the coast of Easter Island, and driven across the intervening tract of ocean to America.

The reader will perceive that there is nothing forced or strained in the supposition I have thus submitted. It is only another supposed case of what we know has occurred thousands of times in the Pacific Ocean—that of an unfortunate vessel being driven far out of her proper course or place by some sudden and violent gale of westerly wind. The distance, also, which Mr. Hill estimates at 2200 miles, is not greater than a Polynesian vessel, especially in the period of the ancient civilization of the islands, might be supposed to traverse with perfect safety, under a strong westerly gale of three or four weeks' duration.

The strength of the gale supposed would necessarily preclude any divergence, either northward or southward, from the direct line of the latitude of Easter Island; and consequently the original landing place of the Polynesians in America would be somewhere near Copiapo, in Chili, in the latitude of that Island.

My theory, therefore, which I am confident I shall succeed in establishing in the following pages, is, that the continent of America was first reached at a period of the highest antiquity in the history of mankind, somewhere near Copiapo, in Chili, by a handful of Polynesians, who had been caught in a sudden and violent gale of westerly wind off Easter Island, in the Southern Pacific, and had crossed the intervening tract of ocean to the American land; and that from these islanders and their descendants the whole Indo-American race of both continents is derived.

Taking it for granted, therefore, for the present, that my theory is well founded, and leaving the proofs and illustrations I shall submit on the subject for the sequel, I would only make the few following preliminary observations.

What, then, I would ask, would be the first object of this handful of Polynesians and their immediate descendants in the unknown land on which they had thus been cast? Why, it would doubtless be to reproduce in their new settlements the whole framework of society, as it existed in Easter Island when they left it, never to return. And considering the evidences of a comparatively high state of civilization, and especially of a wonderful knowledge and control of the mechanical powers which the colossal remains of that island still present on the part of its ancient inhabitants, they would certainly leave evidences of a similar kind, as we shall see in the sequel they have actually done, in the places of their earlier migrations in the unknown land. In process of time, also, parties and individuals of an adventurous spirit would push out into the great

American wilderness and form settlements, from time to time, in all suitable localities, to be afterwards developed in the more eligible into cities and towns. In short, they would just do what Englishmen have been doing in all these Australian colonies from their first settlement to the present day.

And what direction would these explorers be likely to take in their earlier migrations in their new land? Why, the long line of the Andes or Cordilleras, and their vicinity to the Pacific coast, would effectually prevent them from getting to the East, and their lines of migration would therefore be limited to the north and to the south. As islanders and mariners they would probably take possession of such places along the Peruvian coast, to the northward, as would be suitable for the settlement of such a people; and, ascending afterwards to the elevated plains along the base of the mountains, they would form villages and towns, to be afterwards developed, in the course of ages, into the cities of Cuzco and Quito, in Peru. The language, on this subject, of the illustrious philosopher and traveller, Baron Alexander Humboldt, is very remarkable: "In the New World," says that great writer, "at the beginning of its conquest, the natives were collected into great societies only on the ridge of the Cordilleras and the coasts opposite to Asia."* It would be a hopeless task, I conceive, for any of the numerous theorists who refer the original peopling of America to an ancient immigration across Behring's Straits, to explain this extraordinary fact, and to show how these ancient immigrants could ever have got to South America at all. But, on my theory that the forefathers of the Indo-American race passed across the broadest part of the Pacific to America, it is the very necessity of the case that their descendants should be found collected into great societies in the very places where the great philosopher finds and describes them.

The historians of America, Dr. Robertson and Mr. Prescott, both inform us that the Incas of Peru had, among other great works, constructed a public road of upwards of 1500 miles, from

---

* "Humboldt's Travels," vol. III., page 209.

Cuzco to Quito, their two chief cities; and that, every ten or twelve miles along this road, they had erected storehouses to hold provisions and other requisites for the use of the Inca or his officers, and that these storehouses were called *Tambos*. Now, who can doubt but that this word is merely the Polynesian word *taboo*, with a Spanish pronunciation? *Taboo* was the word used by the New Zealanders to designate the storehouses they erected for the preservation of their seed potatoes or other provisions for any particular district. They were *taboo*, or consecrated, and it was death to touch or steal from them. Nay, I am strongly of opinion that my theory will explain the hitherto inexplicable fact of the appearance of the famous Peruvian reformer, Manco Capac, and his wife, who are said to have arrived, somewhere from the westward, in America; for as that which has once occurred may, in similar circumstances, occur again, a similar accident to that which we suppose carried the first party of Polynesians from Easter Island to America, may, after an interval of five hundred, or even a thousand years, have been repeated in the case of another party of unfortunates, including Manco Capac and his wife, when the Polynesian system had developed itself more fully in the island than on the mainland. Neither would it be necessary, on this supposition, that these unfortunates should have landed at Copiapo; for, as the westerly winds of the higher latitudes of the Southern Pacific Ocean are diverted, in more northern latitudes, into southerly winds, through the influence of the Cordilleras, within a hundred leagues of the coast, the second party may have been carried, by these winds, much farther north, towards the Equator.

I have only one other preliminary remark to make on this part of our subject, in regard to the general character of the Indo-American languages spoken in South America down to the Equator. They are all, therefore, as I shall show in the sequel, of a remarkably vocalic character, like those of the Polynesian dialects generally. I have never had an opportunity of seeing the list of words of the language of the Araucanian Indians of Chili, exhibited in the work of Erçilla, the Spanish historian of that country; but the four words of that language, quoted by De Zuniga, viz., *ytayta, biobio, lemolemo, colocolo,* are decidedly Polynesian in their character and aspect, whatever may be their signification. Let the reader compare them with such Polynesian words as " udiudi, korakora, nohinohi, rekereke," and he will doubtless feel it difficult to avoid the conclusion that these languages are derived from the same source, and were originally the same primitive tongue.

With such presumptive evidence of a general affinity between the Polynesian and the Indo-American languages of South America, we can only regard the following assertions of Mr. Marsden, in reference to the language of the South Sea Islands, as entirely gratuitous and contrary to the fact. " To the languages that prevail on the western coast of South America, from whence Easter Island (the 'ultima Thule' of Polynesia) is not greatly remote, the slightest affinity does not appear."* And, again, " Having now attained

---
*Marsden's " Miscell. Works," page 5.

to that extremity of Polynesia which lies the nearest to the western coast of South America, it becomes a natural subject of curiosity to ascertain whether any similarity exists between our great insular language, and those which prevail on the opposite continent. For this purpose specimens are introduced of the Araucanian of Chili, and Kichuan of Peru; upon the slightest comparison of which it will be seen, that neither of these (*which are totally different from each other*) have even the most remote affinity to the Polynesian; and the same may be asserted with respect to the languages spoken on the more northern parts of that extensive region, which I have examined for this object, as far as Nootka Sound and Oonalaska."* And again, " In the *Historia de las Islas Philipinas, por Martinez de Zuniga,* it is stated that, upon examining the words of the language of Chili, which Erçilla mentions in his ' Araucana,' he finds them *bastante conformes* to the Tagala language. It is surprising that, for the sake of supporting a favourite hypothesis, a

---

*" Miscell. Works," page 61.

respectable writer should venture to assert what is directly contrary to the fact."* De Zuniga's assertion is by no means " contrary to the fact;" and it is only *surprising* that Mr. Marsden should have represented it in that light. The Spaniard does not say that the Araucanian words are the same in sound and in signification as Tagalic words—he merely asserts that the former are *bastante conformes*, " strikingly conformable in their character and structure to the latter," an assertion which is somewhat different, and which Mr. Marsden himself would scarcely call in question.

I have quoted Mr. Marsden so frequently and at such length in these pages, that the reader will naturally desire to know who and what he was. I therefore subjoin the following short notice of his history, which I extract from the number of the *American Quarterly Review*, published in Philadelphia, for Sept., 1836:—" Mr. Marsden was born in 1754, in Ireland; and was first employed in the service of the East India Com-

---
*" Miscell. Works," page 61.

pany, at Bencoolen, so long ago as the year 1771. While in that employment (about nine years), he began his investigations into the history of the Malay nation, the most important people of the eastern archipelago. His History of Sumatra, already mentioned, has been translated into other languages; and we have now before us the *third* edition of the English original. This publication immediately brought the author into notice, and he was soon appointed chief secretary to the Board of Admiralty in England. In 1807, he retired from office, with the usual pension of £1500 a year; and—what is particularly worthy of notice, when disinterestedness and public spirit are not the predominant virtues of the age—this enlightened scholar and patriot most liberally relinquished the pension, which he had so well earned by his substantial services to his country. The English journals of that day characterized this noble act as 'a good example which would not be imitated;' a prediction which has been almost literally verified."

To return to our proper subject from this digression—there are other means of ascertaining the affinities of languages besides identity of sound and signification in the corresponding vocables of each. " Languages," says Baron Humboldt, " are much more strongly characterized by their structure and grammatical forms, than by the analogy of their sounds and of their roots ; and this analogy of sounds is sometimes so disfigured in the different dialects of the same tongue, as not to be distinguishable ; for the tribes into which a nation is divided often designate the same objects by words altogether heterogeneous. Hence it follows, that we are easily mistaken if, neglecting the study of the inflexions, and consulting only the roots—for instance, the words which designate the moon, sky, water, and earth—we decide on the absolute difference of two idioms from the simple want of resemblance in sounds."*

" In America," says the eminent traveller— " and this result of the more modern researches is extremely important, with respect to the history of our species,—from the country of the Esquimaux

---

\* " Humboldt's Personal Narrative," vol. iii. p. 252.

to the banks of the Oroonoko, and again from these torrid banks to the frozen climate of the Straits of Magellan, mother-tongues, entirely different with regard to their roots, have, if we may use the expression, the same physiognomy. Striking analogies of grammatical construction are acknowledged, not only in the more perfect languages, as that of the Incas, the Aymara, the Guarani, the Mexican, and the Cora, but also in languages extremely rude. Idioms, the roots of which do not resemble each other more than the roots of the Sclavonian and the Biscayan, have those resemblances of internal mechanism which are found in the Sanscrit, the Persian, the Greek, and the German languages. It is on account of this general analogy of structure—it is because American languages, which have no word in common (the Mexican, for instance, and the Quichua), resemble each other by their organization, and form complete contrasts with the languages of Latin Europe—that the Indians of the missions familiarize themselves more easily with an American idiom, than with that of the metropolis. In the forests of the Oroonoko, I have heard the rudest Indians speak two or three tongues. Savages of different nations often communicate their ideas to each other by an idiom which is not their own."*

* "Personal Narrative," vol. iii. p. 247.

## CHAPTER VI.

UNITY OR IDENTITY OF THE INDO-AMERICAN RACE, FROM LABRADOR AND THE LAKES OF CANADA, TO TIERRA DEL FUEGO AND CAPE HORN.

My authorities for adopting the heading of this chapter, which certain persons may perhaps think unwarranted, are:—

1. The illustrious philosopher and traveller, Humboldt, a man of world-wide fame, especially in all matters connected with America and its native inhabitants.

2. Dr. Von Martius, an eminent Professor in the University of Munich, who, with his colleague Dr. Spix, was sent out to travel in the Brazils early in the present century, in the suite of a Bavarian Princess, the consort elect of Don Pedro, Emperor of the Brazils.

3. Dr. Samuel George Morton, M.D., of Philadelphia, the eminent author of a very learned and scientific work, entitled, "Crania Americana," Philadelphia, 1839.

Humboldt treats his subject—the Indo-Americans, their character and their works—*con amore*. He has evidently a high opinion of the capabilities of the Indo-American people. He pourtrays them in the period of their greatest glory, and describes with much interest and animation the nature and extent of their governments, the magnificent buildings they had erected many ages ago,—of which the stupendous ruins are still the admiration of the world—and the wonderful achievements they had made, with the most inadequate means, in science and art.

Dr. Von Martius views his subject under a very different light. He has evidently imbibed a strong prejudice against the whole Indo-American race, and he follows them, accordingly, into the gloomy forests of the Brazils, where, only, he seems to have seen, or come in contact with them, and where, in entire isolation from the rest of mankind, they seem, from his description, to have lost the essential characteristics of humanity, and to be hastening, by a sort of living death, to their own utter extinction.

Dr. Morton, with wonderful diligence and the highest scientific attainments, collects the skulls of all the tribes of the Indo-American race that have ever inhabited their great continent; both from the receptacles of the dead in the present age, and from the mummy pits of past generations, describing and comparing them with those of the other tribes of mankind, and submitting to his readers the conclusions which his enquiries suggest.

But all these three eminent and highly competent men, however they may differ from each other in certain minor points, agree in this, that they consider the whole Indo-American race one people, and without mixture, from the farthest north to the farthest south of that great continent over which they have been roaming for thousands of years.*

---

\* In the article on America, in the *Encyclopædia Britannica*, I find the following passage, which enables me to add to the great names I have given above, in favour of the unity or identity of the Indo-American race, that of Blumenbach, a philosopher who, it is well known, occupies the first rank in the scientific world. "Physiologists are not at one in their accounts of the characteristics of the aborigines of the new world, nor are they agreed as to whether they should be considered one race, or several. Blumenbach places them all under one class, except the Esquimaux."

"The nations of America," says the illustrious traveller, Humboldt—thereby deciding the question as to the unity and identity of the Indo-American race, authoritatively and at once—"the nations of America, except those which border on the polar circle, form a single race, characterized by the formation of the skull, the colour of the skin, the extreme thinness of the beard, and straight and glossy hair." And again,—" We shall be surprised to find, towards the end of the fifteenth century, in a world which we call new, *those ancient institutions, those religious notions, and that style of building,* which seem in Asia to indicate the very dawn of civilization. The characteristic features of nations, like the internal construction of plants, spread over the surface of the globe, *wear the impression of a primitive type,* notwithstanding the variety produced by the difference of climates, the nature of the soil, and the concurrence of many accidental causes.

A small number of nations, far different from each other,—the Etruscans, the Egyptians, the people of Thibet, and the Aztecs or Mexicans—exhibit striking analogies in their buildings, their religious institutions, their division of time, their cycles of regeneration, and their mystic notions.*

Again,—" It cannot be doubted that the greater part of the nations of America belong to a race of men, who, isolated ever since the infancy of the world from the rest of mankind, exhibit in the nature and diversity of language, in their features and the conformation of their skull, incontestible proofs of an early and complete separation."†

And again,—" I think I discover in the mythology of the Americans, in the style of their paintings, in their languages, and especially in their external conformation,--the descendants of a race of men, which, early separated from the rest of mankind, has followed for a lengthened series of ages a peculiar road in the unfolding of

---

\* "Humboldt's Researches," vol. i, p. 2.
† "Humboldt's Researches," vol. i, p. 250.

its intellectual faculties, and in its tendency towards civilization."*

Such, then, are the matured opinions of that illustrious writer, Baron Alexander Humboldt, in regard to the unity or identity of the Indo-

---

\* "Humboldt's Researches," vol. i, p. 200.

With respect to Humboldt's observation as to the "external conformation" of the Indo-Americans being one of the grounds of his opinion as to the identity of the race and their early separation from the rest of mankind, I would observe that in a work published towards the close of last century, by the elder Blumenbach (*Ueber die Verschiedenheiten im Menschengeschlecht*, On the Radical Distinctions in the Human Species), that eminent naturalist observes:—"Philosophers are now agreed that the character of the hair and the colour of the skin are not sufficient grounds for establishing a radical distinction between different tribes of men." Blumenbach supposes, however, with Dr. Morton, that the conformation of the skull, in the different divisions of the human family, affords the requisite ground for such distinctions, and accordingly divides the family of man into five grand divisions or races, which he considers radically and essentially distinct, viz., the Caucasian or European, the Ethiopic or Negro, the Mongolian or Chinese, the Malayan, and the American. But this division is rather arbitrary, and has not been acquiesced in by ethnologists generally. For my own part, I am strongly of opinion that the Malayan and American should not constitute two distinct divisions of the human family, and Dr. Morton seems to me to be of that opinion himself.

American race. They are all, in his estimation, the same people, sprung from the same source, and separated from the rest of mankind in the very earliest period of the history of man.

The accomplished Bavarian traveller to whom I have already alluded, finding the existence, and the past and present condition, of man in the forests of America a problem too difficult for his own philosophy to solve, has adopted the unphilosophical hypothesis which the Roman historian, Tacitus, had advanced so long before, in regard to the existence of his own German forefathers in the ancient Hercynian forest. Dr. Von Martius believes the Indo-Americans indigenous. He regards them as a race peculiar to the continent they inhabit—an inferior and unfinished specimen of humanity—the abortive effort, perchance, of some ancient Demiurgus, emulous, but yet utterly unable, to copy the noblest work of the Supreme Creator—the Caucasian, or European, man. The German philosopher's description of his unhappy subject is highly interesting, highly eloquent; and, as it serves to form the groundwork of one of the most recently erected superstructures of infidelity, in maintaining that the Indo-American is indigenous, and has no relationship to any other portion of the human race, it may not be unprofitable for the reader to find that that superstructure has no foundation in fact, and that the unhappy objects of the philosopher's commiseration are intimately related in the way of natural descent with another large portion of the family of man.

"The indigenous race of the New World," observes Dr. Von Martius, "is distinguished from all the other nations of the earth, externally by peculiarities of make, but still more, internally, by their state of mind and intellect. The aboriginal American is at once in the incapacity of infancy and unpliancy of old age: he unites the opposite poles of intellectual life. This strange and inexplicable condition has hitherto frustrated almost every attempt to reconcile him completely with the European, to whom he gives way, so as to make him a cheerful and happy member of the community; and it is this, his double nature, which presents the greatest difficulty to science, when she endeavours to investigate his origin and those earlier epochs of his history in which he has, for thousands of years, moved indeed, but made no improvement in his condition. But this is far removed from that natural state of childlike serenity which marked (as an inward voice declares to us, and as the most ancient written documents affirm) the first and purest period of the history of mankind. The men of the *red race*, on the contrary, it must be confessed, do not appear to feel the blessing of a Divine descent, but to have been led by merely animal instinct and tardy steps through a dark Past to their actual cheerless Present. Much, therefore, seems to intimate that the native Americans are not in the first stage of that simple—we might say, physical—development, that they are in a secondary regenerated state.

"We behold in Brazil a thinly scattered population of aboriginal natives, who agree in bodily make, temperament, disposition, manners, customs, and mode of living; but their languages present a truly astonishing discordance. We often meet with one used only by a few individuals connected with each other by relationship who are thus completely isolated, and can hold no communication with any of their other countrymen far and near. Out of the twenty Indians employed as rowers in the boat in which we navigated the streams of the interior, there were often not more than three or four who understood any common language; and we had, before our eyes, the melancholy spectacle of individuals labouring jointly, though entirely isolated with respect to everything which contributes to the satisfaction of the first wants of life. In gloomy silence did these Indians ply the oar together, and join in managing the boat, or in taking their frugal meals; but no common voice or common interest cheered them as they sat beside each other during a journey of several hundred miles, which their various fortunes had called them to perform together."

After mentioning the fact that one hundred and fifty different languages and dialects are spoken in Brazil,* and that more than two hundred and fifty different names of nations, hordes, or tribes, are at present found in that country, Dr. Von Martius observes: "To guide the inquirer through the intricacies of this labyrinth, there is not a vestige of history to afford any clue. Not a ray of tradition, not a war-song nor a funeral-lay can be found to clear away the dark night in which the earlier ages of America are involved." And again, "To the north of the river of Amazons there is an extraordinary number of small

---

\* The case of the Indo-Brazilians, in being broken up into so many different tribes, speaking so many different languages, is not quite so unprecedented as the Bavarian philosopher supposes, as the following quotation will show:—"The negro races who inhabit the mountains of the Malayan peninsula, in the lowest and most abject state of social existence, though numerically few, are divided into a great many distinct tribes, speaking as many different languages. Among the rude and scattered population of the island of Timor, it is believed that not less than forty languages are spoken. On Ende and Flores we have also a multiplicity of languages; and among the cannibal population of Borneo, it is not improbable many hundreds are spoken. Civilization advances as we proceed westward; and in the considerable island of Sambawa there are but five tongues; in the civilized portion of Celebes not more than four; in the great island of Sumatra not above six, and in Java but two."—Crawford's Hist. Ind. Archip., vol. ii., p. 79.

hordes and tribes bearing the most dissimilar appellations, as if the original population, displaced by still more frequent emigrations, wars, and other unknown catastrophes, had here been broken up and split into feebler aggregations. These hordes are found consisting of only one, or at most a few families, entirely cut off from all communication with their neighbours; cautiously concealed in the gloom of their primeval forests, from which they can never issue except when terrified by some external cause; and speaking a highly impoverished and crippled language—the afflicting image of that hapless state in which man oppressed with the curse of his existence, as if striving to fly from himself, shuns the approach of his brother.

"While, in other parts of the world, we see various degrees of intellectual development and retardation simultaneously and proximately occurring—the ever-varying consequences of the changing course of events—the whole aboriginal population of America, on the contrary, exhibits one monotonous poverty of intellect and mental torpor; as if neither internal emotions, nor the impression of external objects, had been able to rouse and release them from their moral inflexibility. This is the more astonishing, as it appears to extend from pole to pole, and applies to the inhabitants of the tropics as well as to the natives of the frozen zones. Yet, this rude and melancholy condition is beyond a doubt, not the first in which the American was placed; it is a degenerate and debased state. Far beyond it, and separated by the obscurity of ages, lies a nobler past, which he once enjoyed, but which can now be only inferred from a few relics. Colossal works of architecture, comparable in extent to the monuments of ancient Egypt (as those of Tiahuanacu on the lake Titicaca, which the Peruvians, as far back as the time of the Spanish conquest, beheld with wonder as the remains of a much more ancient people,—raised, according to tradition, as if by magic, in a single night; and similar creations, scattered in enigmatic fragments, here and there, over both the Americas), bear witness that their inhabitants had, in remote ages, developed a moral power and mental cultivation which have now entirely vanished. A mere semblance of them—an attempt to bring back a period which had long passed by—seems perceptible in the kingdom and institutions of the Incas. In Brazil no such trace of an earlier civilization has yet been discovered; and if it ever existed here, it must have been in a very remotely distant period; yet still, even the condition of the Brazilians, as of every other American people, furnishes proofs that the inhabitants of this New Continent, as it is called, are by no means a modern race, *even supposing we could assume our Christian chronology as a measure for the age and historical development of their country.* This irrefragable evidence is furnished by Nature herself, in the domestic animals and esculent plants by which the aboriginal American is surrounded, and which trace an essential feature in the history of his mental culture. The present state of these productions of nature is a documentary proof, that in America she has been already, for many thousands of years, influenced by the improving and transforming hand of man." After pursuing this idea at considerable length, Dr. Von Martius states his " conviction, that *the first germs of development of the human race in America can be sought nowhere except in that quarter of the globe.*"

" Besides the traces of a primeval, and, in like manner, ante-historic culture of the human race in America, as well as a very early influence on the productions of nature, we may also adduce as a ground for these views, the basis of the present state of natural and civil rights among the aboriginal Americans ; I mean precisely, as before observed, that enigmatical subdivision of the natives into an almost countless multitude of greater and smaller groups, and that almost entire exclusion and excommunication with regard to each other, in which mankind presents its different families to us in America, like the fragments of a vast ruin. The history of the other nations inhabiting the earth furnishes nothing which has any analogy to this.

" This disrupture of all the bands by which

society was anciently held together, accompanied by a Babylonish confusion of tongues multiplied by it—the rude right of force, the never-ending tacit warfare of all against all, springing from that very disrupture—appear to me the most essential, and, as far as history is concerned, the most significant points in the civil condition of the Brazilians, and, in general, of the whole aboriginal population of America. Such a state of society cannot be the consequence of modern revolutions. It indicates, by marks which cannot be overlooked or disputed, the lapse of many ages.

" Long-continued migrations of single nations and tribes have doubtless taken place from a very early period throughout the whole continent of America, and they may have been especially the causes of dismemberment and corruption in the languages, and of a corresponding demoralization of the people. By assuming that only a few leading nations were at first, as was the case with the Tupi people, dispersed like so many rays of light, mingled together, and dissolved, as it were, into each other by mutual collision; and that these migrations, divisions, and subsequent combinations have been continued *for countless ages*, the present state of mankind in America may assuredly be accounted for; but the cause of this singular misdevelopment remains, no less on that account, unknown and enigmatical. Can it be conjectured that some extensive convulsion of nature—some earthquake rending asunder sea and land, such as is reported to have swallowed up the far-famed island of Atalantis—has there swept away the inhabitants in its vortex? Has such a calamity filled the survivors with a terror so monstrous as, handed down from race to race, must have darkened and perplexed their intellects, hardened their hearts, and driven them, as if flying at random from each other, far from the blessings of social life? Have, perchance, burning and destructive suns, or overwhelming floods, threatened the man of the red race with a horrible death by famine, and armed him with a rude and unholy hostility, so that, maddened against himself by atrocious and bloody acts of cannibalism, he has fallen from the godlike dignity for which he was designed, to his present degraded state of darkness? Or is this *inhumanness* the consequence of deeply-rooted preternatural vices, inflicted by the genius of our race (with a severity which, to the eye of a short-sighted observer, appears, throughout all nature, like cruelty) on the innocent as well as the guilty?"

The conclusion which the learned Bavarian draws from these premises is, "that it is impossible entirely to discard the idea of some general defect in the organization of the red race of men, for it is manifest, that it already bears within itself the germ of an early extinction. The Americans, it cannot be doubted, exhibit symptoms of approaching dissolution. Other nations will live, when these unblessed children of the New World have all gone to their final rest in the long sleep of death. Their songs have long ceased to resound; the immortality of their edifices has long been mouldering, and no elevated spirit has revealed itself in any noble effusions from that quarter of the globe. Without being reconciled with the nations of the East, or with their own fortunes, they are already vanishing away: yes, it almost appears as if no other intellectual life were allotted to them, than that of calling forth our painful compassion, as if they existed only for the negative purpose of awakening our astonishment by the spectacle of a whole race of men, the inhabitants of a large portion of the globe, in a state of living decay.

" In fact, the present and future condition of this red race of men, who wander about in their native land, without house or covering—whom the most benevolent and brotherly love despairs of ever providing with a home—is a monstrous and tragical drama, such as no fiction of the poet ever yet presented to our contemplation. A whole race of men is wasting away before the eyes of its commiserating contemporaries; no power of princes, philosophy, or Christianity, can arrest its proudly gloomy progress towards a certain and utter destruction."*

---

* " Von dem Rechtzustande unter der Ureinwohnern Brasiliens." Eine Abhandlung Von Dr. C. F. Ph. Von Martius.—"On the State of Civil and Natural Rights among the Aborigines of the Brazils." Translated by the Rev. G. C. Renouard, B.D.—' Journal of the Royal Geog. Society, vol. ii.' "

In regard to that peculiarity of make, which, in the estimation of Dr. Von Martius, establishes a radical distinction between the Indo-Americans and all the other divisions of the human family, the difference in external appearance between the aborigines of America and the Polynesians is not greater than might have been expected between tribes of mankind derived from the same common source, but placed in circumstances so very different as to climate and modes of life, during a long succession of ages. Captain Basil Hall detected the Malay (i.e., the Polynesian) cast of countenance in the Indians of Acapulco: and I am confident the Bavarian philosopher would have acknowledged the striking resemblance that subsists between the Indo-Brazilian and the New Zealander, if he had ever had an opportunity of instituting the comparison.* At

---

\* I once saw eight Indo-Brazilians, in the harbour of Rio Janeiro, in the month of February, 1823, immediately after the proclamation of the independence of the Brazils. They were the crew of the Emperor Don Pedro's boat; and I am quite sure that if they could have been seen in the streets of Sydney, without knowing beforehand who or what they were, everyone who saw them would have said they were a party of New Zealanders.

the same time it is a well-known fact, that the common domestic animals do not improve, but rather degenerate, in America: and the same unfavourable influence may have had some effect also on the human form.

As an instance of the influence and effect of climate on the human frame, the phenomenon observed by Burckhardt, in his "Travels in Nubia," is deserving of particular attention. That accurate traveller speaks of a tribe of Arabs, called the Shegyia tribe, inhabiting the north of Africa, who retain the Arab features, speak the Arabic language, and trace their descent from the purest Arabian blood, but who are nevertheless as black as negroes. Black Jews are met with in Morocco and in the East Indies; and the genuine descendants of the old Portuguese settlers on the coast of Coromandel are as dark as the Hindoos. In short, there is nothing in the Indo-American peculiarity of make that may not have arisen from the influence of climate and modes of life; and when the absolute identity of that great division of the human race with the South Sea Islanders can be satisfactorily established on so many independent grounds, it is not inconsistent with true philosophy to ascribe the difference in external form and mental character to that influence alone. There is no such difference, however, as we shall afterwards find, between the Polynesians and the Indo-Americans as we have just seen there is between the different tribes of Arabs in the old world. The peculiarity of the Polynesian and Indo-American races is that they retain their peculiar colour in all climates alike, from Labrador to Cape Horn.

But Dr. Von Martius prefers a still graver charge against the Indo-Americans. He regards them as a radically inferior race—inferior in point of intellect to the rest of mankind, and hopelessly irreclaimable. This idea but ill accords with the state of things among the ancient Mexicans and Peruvians at the era of the Spanish conquest, or with the evidences of a still higher state of civilization with which, on his own showing, the American continent still abounds. What other division of the human race would, in similar circumstances, have attained a higher level than the Indo-Americans appear at one time to have actually reached? Had Europe, for instance, been inhabited exclusively either by the Celtic or the Teutonic race for the last three thousand years; had that race been shut out from all communication with the rest of mankind; had they been equally ignorant of letters and of the use of iron; had their only domestic animals been the dog, the turkey, the llama, and the duck, and their only species of grain Indian corn,—I question whether Europe itself would have vied at this moment with ancient Mexico and Peru. But the manifestations of Indian intellect were not confined to central America. The Indian, Philip, who headed a coalition of Indian nations to expel the colonists of New England, about the middle of the seventeenth century, was a hero of the highest accomplishments, and as worthy of a poet as any of the famous warriors of the Iliad: and for a long period after the occupation of their country, the French Canadians had abundant experience of the superior intelligence of the warlike Iroquois. But the atrocities of Cortez, and the robberies of Pizarro, the *auto-da-fe* that was practised on the brave Guatimozin, and the condemnation of his unhappy subjects to the Spanish mines—these and a thousand other acts of injustice, villainy, and oppression, on the part of numerous European intruders, gradually broke the spirit of the Indo-Americans, and reduced them to that state of intellectual debasement and national decay which they now almost uniformly exhibit.

To satisfy ourselves that there was no such mental incapacity and incompetency on the part of the Indo-American race, as the Bavarian philosopher alleges, whatever may have been the causes of their present depression, we have only to consider what they had actually accomplished when they had the whole American continent to themselves. When America was first discovered and colonized by Europeans, the western equatorial regions of that continent were the seat of extensive, flourishing, and powerful empires, the inhabitants of which were well acquainted with the science of government, and had made no inconsiderable progress in the arts of civilization. At a time when the institution of posts was unknown in Europe, it was in full operation in the empire of Mexico; at a time when a public highway was either a relic of Roman greatness, or a sort of nonentity even in England, there were roads of fifteen hundred miles in length in the empire of Peru. The feudal system was as firmly established in these transatlantic kingdoms as in France, and the system of etiquette that regulated the intercourse of the different ranks of society was as complete and as much respected as in the court of Philip the Second. The Peruvians were ignorant of the art of forming an arch, but they had constructed suspension-bridges across frightful ravines; they had no implement of iron, but their forefathers could move blocks of stone as huge as the sphinxes and the Memnons of Egypt. The Mexicans were unacquainted with the art of forming cast-metal pipes, but they had constructed dikes or causeways as compact as those of Holland; and their capital, which was situated in the centre of a salt-water lake, was supplied with a copious stream of fresh water, brought from beyond the lake in an aqueduct of baked clay. They had had no Cadmus to give them an alphabet; but their picture-writing enabled them to preserve the memory of past events, and to transmit it to posterity.

The third of the three eminent authorities to whom I have appealed on the subject of the unity or identity of the Indo-American race is the late Samuel George Morton, Esq., M.D., of Philadelphia.

In the preface of that writer's great work, entitled *Crania Americana,* he thus states the object of the work:—

"Particular attention has been bestowed on the *crania* from the mounds of this country, which have been compared with similar relics derived both from ancient and modern tribes, in order to examine, by the evidence of osteological facts, whether the American aborigines of all epochs have belonged to one race, or a plurality of races."

And the following is the result he gives of his learned and scientific labours :—

"In conclusion, the author is of the opinion that the facts mentioned in this work tend to sustain the following propositions :—

"1st. That the American race differs essentially from all others, not excepting the Mongolians; nor do the feeble analogies of language, and the more obvious ones in civil and religious institutions and the arts, denote anything beyond casual or colonial communication with the Asiatic nations; and even these analogies may perhaps be accounted for, as Humboldt has suggested, in the mere coincidence arising from similar wants and impulses in nations inhabiting similar latitudes.

"2nd. That the American nations, excepting the Polar tribes, are of one race and one species, but of two great families, which resemble each other in physical, but differ in intellectual character.

"3rd. That the cranial remains discovered in the mounds, from Peru to Wisconsin, belong to the same race, and probably to the Toltecan family."*

I had the honour of becoming acquainted with Dr. Morton during a visit I paid to the United States in the year 1840, and in the course of that visit I spent an evening with him in his own house in Philadelphia. Our conversation turned very much on the subject of his own labours, the Indo-American race; and being apprised of his own conclusion on the subject, viz., that the Indo-Americans were all of one race and one species, I took the liberty to ask him what portion of the human race did the Indo-Americans most resemble in their craniological development, when he replied at once and decidedly, *The Polynesian*.

---

* Crania Americana; or, a Comparative View of the Skulls of Various Aboriginal Nations of North and South America. By Samuel George Morton, M.D., London, 1839. Page 260.

## CHAPTER VII.

THE INDO-AMERICANS AND POLYNESIANS ARE ONE AND THE SAME PEOPLE, SPRUNG FROM THE SAME PRIMITIVE STOCK, AND CONNECTED WITH EACH ? MUTUAL TIES OF PARENTAGE AND DESCENT.

I HAVE shown, I think satisfactorily, in a previous chapter, that the separation of the forefathers of the Polynesian nation from the rest of mankind must have taken place in the earliest period of the history of our race, while the earth, so to speak, was still wet with the waters of the deluge.

Various circumstances in the aspect and history of the earlier postdiluvian nations warrant the conclusion that these nations generally had attained a high degree of civilization, and had derived that civilization from one common source.*

---

\* The five books of Moses abound with highly interesting and instructive indications of the state of the arts and sciences among the earlier postdiluvian nations. From these, as well as from existing monuments, it appears that the Egyptians n

In Etruria and in Egypt, in India and in China, and I will add even in the South Sea Islands and in both Americas, we behold the evidences of a primitive civilization, which in some instances had run its course anterior to the age of Homer, but which, at all events, acknowledged no obligation to the wisdom or refinement of the Greeks. The poet Lucretius inquires why there are no poems of an earlier date than the siege of Troy, and infers that as no poems of an earlier period have been preserved, it has been because none were

---

particular had made very great progress in civilization at an early period after the deluge; but the aspect of things exhibited in the books of Moses indicates a *general*, and by no means inconsiderable, advance in civilization. The use of money, for instance, was well known in the days of Abraham; and caravans of merchants already traversed the Arabian desert, exchanging the productions of one country for those of another. Chariots armed with scythes were used in the Canaanitish wars. Walled cities with locks and keys were numerous. There were surveyors in Joshua's army, who prepared a general chart of the land of Canaan; and the city of *Kirjathsepher*, (the city of the book,) which was anciently called *Debir*, (a word of similar import,) was in all likelihood the seat of an academy or college. In short, the general aspect of society in these primitive times indicates great progress in civilization.

written. But we may rest assured that poetry was not the invention of Orpheus, or of Hesiod, or of Homer. If *the harp and the organ*—these antediluvian inventions of Jubal—were made to "discourse sweet music" in the cities of Cain, we may conclude with absolute certainty, that *the daughters of men* would link with their dulcet sounds the inspirations of poetry and the symphonies of song.

But if the antediluvians were not barbarians, neither were those eight persons that survived the deluge, and landed on the mountains of Armenia from that ancient vessel which was destined to preserve the relics of one world and the germ of another. Antecedently to all historical evidence of the fact, we should be warranted in supposing that Noah and his sons would preserve a knowledge of the arts that flourished, and of the sciences that were cultivated, in the antediluvian world; and that they would exhibit in their earliest postdiluvian settlements the forms and features of antediluvian civilization. But we are not left to the uncertainty of mere conjecture on this point: for the first act of the liberated occupant of the ark was to cultivate the vine, and the earliest effort of the combined labour of his offspring was *to build a city and a tower whose top should reach the heavens.* " The wisdom of the Egyptians "—-the most ancient and the most famous of the postdiluvian nations, and "the excellency of the Chaldees"—the illustrious contemporaries of the Pharaohs—were, doubtless, the transcript of antediluvian science and of antediluvian refinement: for as surely as the forefathers of the New Zealand nation would import the arts and the institutions of their native isle into that distant island, in whatever manner they had reached its solitary shore, and would erect in their new settlement a framework of society and of civilization exactly similar to the one which was still fresh in their recollection, so surely would the earliest of the postdiluvian nations endeavour to remodel society, in all its parts and in all its relations, agreeably to the fashion of the world that had passed so recently away.

In short, as emigration tended greatly to the eastward in these primitive times, there is reason to believe that the forefathers of the great Malayan nation had arrived and settled in Eastern Asia and the isles adjacent, at a period coeval with the origin and establishment of the Egyptian empire in the west: and that the numerous islands of the Indian Archipelago were traversed in all directions by the beautifully-carved galleys of that maritime people long before Agamemnon and his brother chiefs had conducted their hordes of semi-barbarous Greeks to the siege and pillage of Troy.

I have already observed, that the earliest effort of the combined labour of the postdiluvian inhabitants of the earth was *to build a city and a tower whose top should reach the heavens.*

Whether the ostensible object of the architects of the tower of Babel—which it is allowed on all hands was a pyramid—was to prepare a suitable mausoleum for the mouldering remains of departed greatness, or to rear a *high place* for the worship of the Divinity, the real object of its projector is sufficiently obvious from the sacred narrative. The building was evidently intended to subserve the purposes of personal ambition—to concentrate and to enslave the rapidly increasing and extending population of the recently deluged world; in short, to pave the way for the establishment of a universal and despotic monarchy. And what could possibly have suggested so singular a method of effecting such an object, but that the plan had been adopted and been found successful before? In short, there is reason to believe that such towers as the tower of Babel were the proud distinctions of the metropolitan cities of the antediluvian world,—the favourite appendages of antediluvian royalty—the usual evidences and effects of antediluvian despotism. For *there were giants*, i.e., men of prodigious ambition—*men of renown in those days*—doubtless the Napoleons and the Alexanders of the antediluvian world.

But whether the tower of Babel was itself the transcript of antediluvian architecture or not, there is no question as to its having set the fashion to all those postdiluvian tribes that diverged to the eastward and westward from the plain of Shinar—for the fashion in architecture in the earlier postdiluvian ages was certainly pyramidal and colossal; and the prevalence of that style of building in the architectural remains of any country is accordingly a sure indication of the remotest antiquity. The pyramids of Egypt have been so famous in all past ages, and the durable materials of which they have been constructed have so long resisted the ravages of time, that we are apt to forget that Egypt is not the only country in which such stupendous and apparently useless structures have been reared. The ancient Etrurians, whose elegantly formed vases were occasionally dug up in the neighbourhood of Rome in the age of Augustus, and were then esteemed as precious a relic of antiquity as a Grecian statue in the present age, had evidently imbibed their civilization at the same fountain as the ancient Egyptians; for they also constructed pyramids, though of less durable materials than the pyramids of Egypt. Varro speaks of four Etrurian pyramids in the city of Clusium—the burial place of King Porsenna, one of the earliest and most formidable of the enemies of the Romans—of upwards of eighty French metres, or about two hundred and fifty English feet, in perpendicular height. Pyramids of a remote antiquity have also been found in India and in China ; and the Indian pagoda and the pyramidal forms which the Chinese and the Indo-Chinese nations—those determined sticklers for the fashions of bygone time—still affect in their public buildings, are doubtless to be referred to the same primitive source.

Before proceeding with the proof of my case, as stated in the title of this chapter, I shall now present the reader with the remarkable account not only of a house, but of a city of the pyramidal and colossal period, still standing exactly as it did four thousand years ago.

The Rev. Dr. Porter, formerly a missionary from the Presbyterian Church of Ireland, in Damascus, and now a Professor in the General Assembly's College, in Belfast, having visited, during his stay in the East, the *Giant Cities of Bashan*, gives us the following account of one in which he spent a night, as illustrative of the colossal style of architecture prevalent in these cities four thousand years ago.

"The house seemed to have undergone little change from the time its old master had left it; and yet the thick nitrous crust on the floor showed that it had been deserted for long ages. The walls were perfect, nearly five feet thick, built of large blocks of hewn stones, *without lime or cement of any kind*. The roof was formed of large slabs of the same black basalt, lying as regularly, and jointed as closely, as if the workman had only just completed them. They measured twelve feet in length, eighteen inches in breadth, and six inches in thickness. The end rested on a plain stone cornice, projecting about a foot from each side wall. The chamber was twenty feet long, twelve wide, and ten high. The outer door was a slab of stone four and a half feet high, four wide, and eight inches thick. It hung upon pivots, formed of projecting parts of the slab, working in sockets in the lintel and threshold; and though so massive, I was able to open and shut it with ease. At one end of the room was a small window, with a stone shutter. An inner door, also of stone, but of finer workmanship, and not quite so heavy as the other, admitted to a chamber of the same size and appearance. From it a much larger door communicated with a third chamber, to which there was a descent by a flight of stone steps. This was a spacious hall, equal in width to the two rooms, and about twenty-five feet long by twenty high. A semicircular arch was thrown across it, supporting the stone roof; and a gate, so large that camels could pass in and out, opened on the street. The gate was of stone, and in its place; but some rubbish had accumulated on the threshold, and it appeared to have been open for ages. Here our horses were comfortably installed. Such were the internal arrangements of this old mansion. It had only one story; and its ample, massive style of architecture gave evidence of a very remote antiquity.

On a large stone which formed the lintel of the gateway, there was a Greek inscription, but it was so high up, and my light so faint, that I was unable to decipher it, though I could see that the letters were of the old style. It is probably the same which was copied by Burckhardt, and which bears a date apparently equivalent to the year before Christ 306!

"Owing to the darkness of the night, and the shortness of our stay, I was unable to ascertain, from personal observation, the extent of Burak, or the character of its buildings; but the men who gathered round me, when I returned to my chamber, had often visited it. They said the houses were all like the one we occupied, only some smaller, and a few larger, but there were no great buildings. Burak stands on the north-east corner of the Lejah, and was therefore one of the frontier towns of ancient Argob. It is built upon rocks, and encompassed by rocks so wild and rugged as to render it a natural fortress."*

---

\* The Giant Cities of Bashan. London, 1868. Pages 26, 27.

Such was the state of things as to domestic architecture in the earlier ages of the post-diluvian world, when the forefathers of the Polynesian nation were separated for ever from the rest of mankind, and their long migrations in all parts of the Pacific Ocean commenced. Some unfortunate Malayan galley, passing in all probability from one island to another of the Philippine group, being caught suddenly by a violent westerly gale, and carried, without the slightest hope of ever finding its way back, to some remote island in the Western Pacific, would there form its tiny settlement, and thereby give its first population to that vast ocean.

I have also shewn, in the previous chapters of this volume, how these unfortunates and their descendants have, during the long series of past ages, spread themselves over the multitude of the isles of the vast Pacific Ocean, and at last reached the west coast of South America, somewhere near Copiapo, in the Republic of Chili. And I am now to show that the Indo-American race in both continents of America are the lineal descendants of the handful of famished Polynesians who landed so many ages ago from their ancient vessel on that solitary shore.

I do so, therefore, in the first place, from the identity of their architectural remains, many of which exhibit the evidences of the highest antiquity. The very remarkable remains of this kind which we find both in Polynesia and in Indo-America consist of temples, as they are called, pyramids, terraces or platforms, and colossal statues.

1st.—Temples. Dr. Robertson, the historian of America, had evidently formed a very unfavourable opinion both of the Indo-Americans, and of their works and remains, probably from his comparative inacquaintance with the subject; for the noble volumes of Humboldt—his Personal Narrative and Researches—were not published till after Dr. Robertson's death, which took place in 1793.

The following is Dr. Robertson's somewhat disparaging description of the great Temple of Mexico.

"The great Temple (or Teocalli) of Mexico, the most famous in New Spain, which has been represented as a magnificent building, raised to such a height that the ascent to it was by a flight of a hundred and fourteen steps, was a solid mass of earth, of a square form, faced partly with stone. Its base on each side extended ninety feet, and decreasing gradually as it advanced in height, it terminated in a quadrangle of about thirty feet, where were placed a shrine of the deity, and two altars on which the victims were sacrificed. All the other celebrated temples of New Spain exactly resembled that of Mexico."*

Perfectly identical in its plan, and in the style of its architecture with the Temple of Mexico, is that of Copan, one of the recently discovered Indo-American cities of Yucatan, in central America. The following is the description of that building, by Mr. Stephens, the American Traveller.

"COPAN.

"This temple is an oblong enclosure. The front or river wall extends in a right line north

---

* Robertson's History of America. Book VII., 228.

and south six hundred and twenty-four feet, and it is from sixty to ninety feet in height. It is made of cut stones, from three to six feet in length, and a foot and a half in breadth. In many places the stones have been thrown down by bushes growing out of the crevices, and in one place there is a small opening, from which the ruins are sometimes called by the Indians Las Ventanas, or the windows. The other three sides consist of ranges of steps and pyramidal structures, rising from thirty to one hundred and forty feet on the slope. The whole line of survey is two thousand eight hundred and sixty-six feet, which though gigantic and extraordinary for a ruined structure of the aborigines, that the reader's imagination may not mislead him, I consider it necessary to say, it is not so large as the base of the great pyramid of Ghizeh."*

But the reader will, doubtless, be astonished to find that these two ancient Indo-American temples are exactly on the same plan as that of

---

* Stephen's Incidents of Travel in Central America, Chiapas and Yucatan. Vol. I. 133.

the Temple (or Marae) of Atehuru, in Tahiti, of which I subjoin the following description.

### TEMPLE (OR MARAE) OF ATEHURU, IN TAHITI.

"The form of the interior or area of these temples was frequently that of a square, or parallelogram, the sides of which extend to forty or fifty feet. Two sides of this space were enclosed by a high stone wall; the front was protected by a low fence, and opposite a solid pyramidal structure was raised, in front of which the images were kept, and the altars fixed. These piles were often immense. That which formed one side of the square of the large temple in Atehuru was two hundred and seventy feet long, ninety feet wide at the base, and fifty feet high, being at the summit one hundred and eighty feet long, and six wide. A flight of steps led to its summit, the bottom step was six feet high. The outer stones of the pyramid, composed of coral and basalt, were laid with great care, and hewn or squared with immense labour, especially the tiavâ or corner stones. Within the enclosure, the houses of the priests and the temples of the idols were erected. Ruins of temples are found in every situation. On the summit of a hill, as at Maeva, where the ruins of Tané's temple, one hundred and twenty feet square, enclosed with high walls, is still standing, almost entire."*

We have a somewhat similar account of the temples, or *heiaus*, as they were there called, of the Hawaiian or Sandwich Islands.

"Temples, or *heiaus*, were commonly erected upon hills, or near the sea, and formed conspicuous objects in the landscapes. They were works of great labour, built of loose stones, with sufficient skill to form compact walls. The usual form was an irregular parallelogram. That of Kawaikai or Hawaii, was 224 feet long, and 100 feet wide, with walls twelve feet thick at the base, from eight to twenty feet high, and two to six feet wide at the top, which being well paved with smooth stones, formed, when in repair, a pleasant walk. The entrance was nar-

---

* Polynesian Reseaches. I., 340, 341.

row, between two high walls. The interior was divided into terraces, the upper one paved with flat stones. The south end constituted an inner court, and was the most sacred place. The sacrificial altar was near the entrance to this court. Only the high chiefs and priests were allowed to reside within the precincts of the temple."*

Here then we have specimen temples of the Polynesians on the one hand, and the Indo-Americans on the other, perfectly identical in their plans and details, but altogether unlike any religious edifices that had ever been seen or heard of in the old world for two or three thousand years past. A parallelogram, of larger or smaller dimensions, as it suited the particular case, with a low fence in front, a strong wall to the right and left, enclosing the area of the temple, and a long flight of steps to the summit or platform of a truncated pyramidal building, right opposite, but without

---

* Jarvis's History of the Hawaiian Islands. Chapter II., page 50.

a roof—such was the *Marai* of the Polynesians, and the Teocalli of the Indo-Americans. It is scarcely proper to call these structures temples; but they were each like a parish church in our own country—the place of worship, and especially the place of sacrifice, for the surrounding district.

But we are not altogether without the means of identifying the Polynesian *Marai* and the Indo-American *Teocalli* with the places of worship, and especially the places of sacrifice, of the earlier postdiluvian nations. It is matter of history that there was some kind of worship, some religious observances, celebrated on what were called *high places* in the earliest postdiluvian times. Mr. Mitford, in his history of Greece, observes that the great antiquity of the writings of Homer may be inferred from the fact that he makes no mention either of temples or of images. So early, indeed, was this kind of worship practised in the postdiluvian ages, that it were not unreasonable to suppose that it had been practised in the antediluvian world, and reproduced in the earlier postdiluvian ages, from the reminiscences of the eight survivors of the deluge. Originally the worship celebrated on these "high places" was in honour of the one living and true God; afterwards, however, and at a very early period, it was offered to numberless heathen divinities, and was accompanied with all manner of abominable practices.

So late as the times of Samuel, and even of Solomon, we read of such "high places" being devoted to the worship of the true God. "And Samuel answered Saul, and said, I am the Seer, go up before me unto the 'high place,' for ye shall eat with me to-day."* And again. "And Solomon, and all the congregation with him, went to the 'high place' that was at Gibeon."†

But so infamous had the "high places" of Palestine become at an early period that the Israelites were divinely commanded, on their taking possession of the Holy Land, utterly to destroy them. "Then ye shall drive out all the inhabitants of the land from before you, and destroy all their pictures, and destroy all their molten images,

---

* 1 Samuel ix. 19.    † 2 Samuel i. 3.

and quite pluck down all their 'high places.'\*
"For they provoked Him to anger with their *high places*, and moved Him to jealousy *with their graven images.*" †

Notwithstanding this prohibition, however, the people of Israel were so strongly attached to the worship of the "high places" that even their reforming monarchs were quite unsuccessful in their efforts to put it down. Thus in the case of King Asa. "But the 'high places' were not taken away out of Israel; nevertheless, the heart of Asa was perfect all his days."‡

We have no information, either in sacred or profane history, as to the form and character of these "high places" of the ancients; but I have no doubt whatever that they were exactly of the form and character represented to us in the Polynesian *Marai*, and the Indo-American *Teocalli*. Taking it for granted, therefore, for the reasons I have stated above, that the emigration to the eastward from the plain of Shinar

---

\* Numbers xxxiii. 52.   † Psalm lxxviii. 58.
‡ 2 Chronicles xv. 17.

took place at a very early period after the deluge, when the knowledge and worship of the true God was still cherished and taught by the preachers of righteousness who succeeded Noah and his sons, it is natural to suppose that these emigrants would, from time to time, erect high places exactly similar to those in use among their fathers, in all their places of settlement on their way across the continent of Asia, till they reached the Indian Archipelago and the Philippine Islands. And as the handful of Malays who, we suppose, were accidentally driven by a strong westerly gale into the boundless Pacific, were not barbarians, but in a comparatively high state of civilization, and well acquainted with the use of the mechanical powers, the form and character of the "high places" of their time would be deeply photographed upon their minds, and the sublime idea of one great Spirit, all powerful, but invisible to men, would be impressed upon their hearts; the religious edifice to be reproduced from time to time in buildings of a precisely similar form and character, first in the multitude of the isles of the vast

Pacific Ocean, and afterwards in the continent of America; and the spiritual idea to be treasured up in their hearts and taught to their posterity. To suppose that the North American Indian could have excogitated for himself the idea of one Great Spirit, controlling the universe, but invisible to men, is something I cannot believe; especially as such an idea had never been attained by the sages of Greece and of Rome. But I can easily conceive of it as a fragment of Divine Revelation impressed upon the minds of the forefathers of the Polynesian nation, and carried by them and their descendants across the Pacific and to both continents of America. At all events, there is no question as to the fact of there being such an impression on the American mind. "The Indians of the forest," says Baron Humboldt, "when they visit occasionally the missions, conceive with difficulty the idea of a temple or an image. 'These good people,' said the missionary, 'like only processions in the open air.' When I last celebrated the patron festival of my village, that of San Antonio, the Indians of Inirida were present at mass. 'Your God,' said they to me, 'keeps himself shut up in a house, as if he were old and infirm: ours is in the forest, in the fields, and on the mountains of Sipapu, whence the rains come.'"*

The frontispiece of this work is a copy of the painting of a Mexican Teocalli, or patriarchal "high place," painted by a M. Dupaix, an eminent French artist, by command of the King of Spain, and contained in Volume IV. of Lord Kingsborough's "Monuments of Mexico," a copy of which is in the Sydney University Library.

The other items in which the architectural remains of the Polynesians and Indo-Americans indicate and prove the identity of these two nations, are terraces, colossal statues, and pyramids.

Perhaps the most remarkable, as it is doubtless the most ancient, instance of the terraces of the Polynesians, is that of the Marquesas group, in the Southern Pacific, of which the following account is given us by Herman Melville, an

---

\* Humboldt's Narrative, vol. v. p. 273.

intelligent and trustworthy American, who resided for some time in the Marquesas.

"At the base of one of the mountains, and surrounded on all sides by dense groves, a series of vast terraces of stone rises step by step for a considerable distance up the hill side. These terraces cannot be less than 100 yards in length, and 20 in width. Their magnitude, however, is less striking than the immense size of the blocks composing them. Some of the stones, of an oblong shape, are from ten to fifteen feet in length, and five or six feet thick. Their sides are quite smooth, but though square, and of pretty regular formation, they bear no mark of the chisel. They are laid together without cement, and here and there show gaps between. The topmost terrace and the lower one are somewhat peculiar in their construction. They have both a quadrangular depression in the centre, leaving the rest of the terrace elevated several feet above it. In the intervals of the stones immense trees have taken root, and their broad boughs stretch far over, and, interlacing together, support a canopy almost impenetrable to the sun. Overgrowing a greater part of them, and climbing from one to another, is a wilderness of vines, in whose sinewy embrace many of the stones lie half hidden, while in some places a thick growth of bushes entirely covers them. There is a wild pathway which obliquely crosses two of these terraces; and so profound is the shade, so dense the vegetation, that a stranger to the place might pass along it without being aware of their existence. As I gazed upon this monument, doubtless the work of an extinct and forgotten race, thus buried in the green nook of an island at the end of the earth, the existence of which was yesterday unknown, a stronger feeling of awe came over me than if I had stood musing at the mighty base of the Pyramid of Cheops. There are no inscriptions, no sculpture, no clue by which to conjecture its history—nothing but dumb stones. How many generations of those majestic trees which now overshadow them have grown and flourished and decayed since they were first erected."*

---

\* Melville's Marquesas Islands, chapter 21.

Captain Cook describes a somewhat similar terrace in Easter Island, of which he regards the workmanship as equal to that of any English workman.* And in his description of the ruins of the ancient city of Copan, in Central America, Mr. Stephens informs us that there "is a confused range of terraces running all into the forest, ornamented with death's heads, some of which are still in position, and others lying about, as they have fallen or been thrown down."† And as to the colossal statues, consisting of immense blocks of stone, and standing either singly or in groups, there is precisely the same thing to be seen in Easter Island, in Polynesia, as in Copan, Palenque, and Uxmal, in Central America. The only difference is, that while in Easter Island these colossal statues are rough-hewn from the quarry, and the sculpture of an inferior character, those of the cities of Central America are polished

---

\* Page 90.

† Incidents of Travel in Central America, Chiapas, and Yucatan, Vol. I., 138. By John L. Stephens, Author of Incidents of Travel in Egypt, Arabia Petraea, and the Holy Land. London, 1846.

and sculptured in the highest style of art. Of this difference, however, there is the easiest explanation; for while in Easter Island the statues are rough and unpolished, as one would anticipate in so limited a space for development, and in the infancy of the nation, those of the cities of Central America were erected in the midst of large communities, and in the highest style of art of which their peculiar civilization was susceptible. For I quite agree with Mr. Stephens in regarding the ruined cities of Central America as comparatively modern erections; some of them, as Uxmal for instance, having been, in all likelihood, inhabited down to the era of the Spanish conquest. For there are actually wooden lintels still remaining in the palace of Uxmal, while the use of cement and stucco, comparatively recent inventions, which are used in these buildings, was unheard of and unknown in the era of the more ancient erections, both of Polynesia and of Indo-America. As in the Giant Cities of Bashan, described by Dr. Porter, there was no cement of any kind used in the colossal terraces of the Marquesas Islands, or in the colossal and pyramidal buildings at the Lake of Titicaca, in Peru, both of which must therefore be referred to a period of the remotest antiquity. In these Peruvian buildings there are stones which have been polished and placed by the ancient architect of upwards of thirty feet in length; the protuberances of one stone having been fitted with incredible labour into the natural hollows of the other.

The pyramidal erections of the Polynesians were confined almost exclusively to their temples, although from what Lord Anson or his historiographer relates of the island of Tinian, it would seem that they sometimes erected rows of small pyramids, like those we shall find presently in the valleys of Mexico. Humboldt's remarks on this subject are profoundly interesting, and contrasted with what we find recorded of the Polynesian temples, strongly prove the identity of the two nations.

" Among those swarms of nations, which, from the seventh to the twelfth century of the

Christian era, successively inhabited the country of Mexico, five are enumerated,—the Toltecks, the Cicimecks, the Acolhuans, the Tlascaltecks, and the Aztecks,—who, notwithstanding their political divisions, spoke the same language, followed the same worship, and built pyramidal edifices, which they regarded as *Teocallis*, that is to say, the houses of their gods. These edifices were all of the same form, though of very different dimensions; they were pyramids, with several terraces, and the sides of which stood exactly in the direction of the meridian, and the parallel of the place. The teocalli was raised in the midst of a square and walled enclosure, which, somewhat like the περίβολος of the Greeks, contained gardens, fountains, the dwellings of the priests, and sometimes arsenals; since each house of a Mexican divinity, like the ancient temple of Baal-Berith, built by Abimelech, was a strong place. A great staircase led to the top of the truncated pyramid; and on the summit of the platform were one or two chapels, built like towers, which contained the colossal idols of the divinity to whom the teocalli was dedicated. This part of the edifice must be considered as the most consecrated place; like the ναὸς, or rather the στέγος, of the Grecian temples: it was there also that the priests kept up the sacred fire. From the peculiar construction of the edifice we have just described, the priest who offered the sacrifice was seen by a great mass of the people at the same time: the procession of the *teopixqui*, ascending or descending the staircase of the pyramid, was beheld at a considerable distance. The inside of the edifice was the burial-place of the kings and principal personages of Mexico. It is impossible to read the descriptions which Herodotus and Diodorus Siculus have left us of the temple of Jupiter Belus, without being struck with the resemblance of that Babylonian monument to the teocallis of Anahuac."*

"At the period when the Mexicans, or Aztecks, took possession, in the year 1190, of the equinoctial region of New Spain, they already found

---

* "Humboldt's Researches," vol. i., p. 82.

the pyramidal monuments of Teotihuacan, of Cholula, or Cholollan, and of Papantla. They attributed these great edifices to the Toltecks, a powerful and civilized nation, who inhabited Mexico five hundred years earlier, who made use of hieroglyphical characters, who computed the year more precisely, and had a more exact chronology than the greater part of the people of the old continent. The Aztecks knew not with certainty what tribe had inhabited the country of Anahuac before the Toltecks; and consequently the belief that the houses of the deity of Teotihuacan and of Cholollan was the work of the Toltecks, assigned them the highest antiquity they could conceive."*

" The group of the pyramids of Teotihuacan is in the valley of Mexico, eight leagues north-east from the capital, in a plain that bears the name of Micoatl, or the *path of the dead.* There are two large pyramids dedicated to the sun (Tonatiuh) and to the moon (Meztli); and these are surrounded by several hundreds of small pyramids,

---

\* " Humboldt's Researches," vol. i., p. 83.

which form streets in exact lines from north to south, and from east to west. Of these two great teocallis, one is fifty-five metres (or one hundred and eighty feet), the other forty-four metres (or one hundred and forty-five feet) in perpendicular height. The basis of the first is two hundred and eight metres (or six hundred and seventy-six feet) in length; whence it results that it is higher than the Mycerinus, or third of the three great pyramids of Ghiza in Egypt, and the length of its base nearly equal to that of Cephrenes. The small pyramids, which surround the great houses of the Sun and the Moon, are scarcely nine or ten metres high; and served, according to the tradition of the natives, as burial-places for the chiefs of the tribes. Around the Cheops and the Mycerinus in Egypt there are eight small pyramids, placed with symmetry, and parallel to the fronts of the greater. The two teocallis of Teotihuacan had four principal stories, each of which was subdivided into steps, the edges of which are still to be distinguished. The nucleus is composed of clay mixed with small stones; and it is encased by a thick wall of tezontli, or porous amygdaloid. This construction recalls to mind that of one of the Egyptian pyramids of Sakharah, which has six stories; and which, according to Pocock, is a mass of pebbles and yellow mortar, covered on the outside with rough stones. On the top of the great Mexican teocallis were two colossal statues of the Sun and Moon; they were of stone, and covered with plates of gold, of which they were stripped by the soldiers of Cortez."

The pyramid of Papantla is of much smaller dimensions, but "is built entirely with hewn stones of an extraordinary size, and very beautifully and regularly shaped: three staircases lead to the top. The covering of its steps is decorated with hieroglyphical sculptures and small niches, which are arranged with great symmetry."

But "the greatest, most ancient, and most celebrated of the whole of the pyramidal monuments of Anahuac is the teocalli of Cholula. It is called in the present day the *mountain made by the hand of man* (monte hecho a manos). At a distance it has the aspect of a natural hill covered with vegetation. The teocalli of Cholula has four stories, all of equal height. It appears to have been constructed exactly in the direction of the four cardinal points; but as the edges of the stories are not very distinct, it is difficult to ascertain their primitive direction. This pyramidical monument has a broader basis than that of any other edifice of the same kind in the old continent. I measured it carefully, and ascertained that its perpendicular height is only fifty metres (or one hundred and sixty-two feet), but that each side of its basis is four hundred and thirty-nine metres (or fourteen hundred and twenty-six feet) in length. The basis of the pyramid of Cholula is twice as broad as that of Cheops; but its height is very little more than that of the pyramid of Mycerinus."\*

"We have above remarked the great similarity of construction between the Mexican teocallis and the temple of Bel, or Belus, at Babylon. This analogy had already struck Mr. Zoega, though he

---

\* Humboldt's Researches," vol. i., p. 89.

had been unable to procure but very incomplete descriptions of the group of the pyramids of Teotihuacan. According to Herodotus, who visited Babylon, and saw the temple of Belus, this pyramidal monument had eight stories. It was a stadium (one hundred and eighty-three metres, or five hundred and ninety-five feet) high, and the breadth of the basis was equal to its height. The outer wall, which surrounded it, was two stadia square. The pyramid was built of brick and asphaltum. A temple was erected on its top, and another at its basis." " In the Mexican teocallis, as in the temple of Belus, the lower temple was distinguished from the one on the platform of the pyramid."*

I cannot refrain from inserting, in this part of our subject, in connection with Humboldt's very interesting description of the pyramids of Mexico, the following account of a "Pyramidal Monument in China," from "Ochterlony's Account of the War in that country," page 458, as illustrative of the identity of the style and character of the

---

* " Humboldt's Researches," vol. i., p. 99.

architecture of all the earlier postdiluvian nations in all parts of the world.

### PYRAMIDAL MONUMENT IN CHINA.

" The road (from Nanking) runs parallel with the walls of the Tartar city, until it reaches a rising ground opposite the principal gate, where is situated a magnificent Chinese tomb, representing the raised Cenotaph, usually seen in their burial places. The style of the architecture is massive and striking. It is situated at the extremity of a fine broad road, enclosed between the ramparts, which is paved with large smooth slabs of a dark-coloured limestone, of which material the building itself is constructed. Its form is that of a truncated quadrangular pyramid, about 250 feet long, 180 high, and 160 broad, bearing on its summit an enclosed, but roofless building, in each of whose four walls a handsome arch is twined, opening to the cardinal points; the whole forming a monument so decidedly Egyptian in its style and outline that the traveller, were he able to exclude from his view the surrounding objects, might fancy himself wandering among the ruins of Luxor or Thebes.

There are various customs and practices unknown among other nations, but common alike to the Polynesians and Indo-Americans that proclaim them to be one people.

The first of these is the horrible practice of offering human sacrifices—the victims, who were generally indicated by the priests, if not prisoners of war, being sacrificed on the altar on the summit of their *Marais* or *Teocallis*. This horrid practice doubtless obtained in many extinct nations. Tacitus informs us that it was in use among the ancient Germans,[*] while its prevalence among the ancient Celts, under the reign of the Druids, is matter of notoriety.[†] The question of

---

[*] Stato tempore, in silvam, auguriis patrum et prisca formidine sacram, omnes ejusdem sanguinis populi legationibus coeunt, cæsoque publice homine celebrant barbari ritus horrenda primordia."—Tacit. de Morib. Germ.

[†] The stated time alluded to by Tacitus was called *Beltan* by the ancient Celtic inhabitants of Scotland, by whom a similar practice was annually observed. The word, which is still used in Scotland to signify a term in the year, is a corruption, I have been given to understand, of the Celtic words *Bel-teyn*, "the fire of Bel, Baal, or Belus," the victim being first killed and then consumed by fire.

the king of Moab, "Shall I give my first-born for my transgression, the fruit of my body for the sin of my soul?" and the whole hecatombs of victims* that were offered up in Sicily after the battle of Himera by the Carthaginian general, Hannibal the elder, to the manes of his grandfather Hamilcar, who had been defeated and slain by the Sicilians under Gelon about fifty years before, attest its frequency among the ancient Phœnicians; while the story of Iphigenia perhaps indicates its prevalence among the ancient Pelasgi in the isles of Greece. But in no other part of the world was the practice ever so prevalent, or characterised by such multitudes of victims, as in the South Sea Islands and among the Indo-Americans of Mexico. On the death of the Incas, and of other eminent persons in Peru, a considerable number of their attendants were put to death, and interred around their graves (or tombs) that they might appear in the next world with their former dignity, and be served with the same respect. On the death of Huana Capac, the most powerful of their mon-

---

* The number sacrificed was 3000. B.C. 410.

archs, or Incas, above a thousand victims were doomed to accompany him to the tomb.* And during the siege of Mexico, which was bravely defended by the natives, two or three of the soldiers of Cortez, having been taken prisoners by the Mexicans, were sacrificed on the summit of the great Temple of Mexico, in sight of their sorrowing countrymen.

2. The second of the singular customs that obtain equally among Polynesians and Indo-Americans is their mode of disposing of the dead. During my first visit to New Zealand, in the year 1839, I happened to visit the cemetery of the native village of Kororadika, in the Bay of Islands, in which, instead of graves and tumuli, I found a number of stages or trestles, from two to three feet high, on which the bodies of the dead, which had been wrapped up in mats, were left to putrefy in the open air. I happened to visit the United States during the following year, and became acquainted in New York with the family of a Mr. Catlin, who had spent many years among the

---

* Robertson's History of America. Book VII., p. 237.

Indian tribes of North America, and who was then in England, exhibiting the collections he had made among these tribes, in the Egyptian Hall in London. On my return to England, I made it my business to see Mr. Catlin's exhibition; and among the paintings he had drawn of Indian scenes, there was one of a Mandan village in Upper Missouri, a tribe which was two thousand strong at his first visit to that part of the country, but had been quite annihilated by small pox during the interval. There was nothing remarkable in the appearance of the village; but that of the cemetery attached to it struck me exceedingly at the moment, for it was exactly similar to what I had seen so shortly before in the village of Kororadika, in New Zealand—a series of trestles or stages, on which the bodies of the dead, wrapped up in the skins of wild beasts, had been left to putrefy in the open air.

This mode of disposing of the dead seems to have been extensively prevalent among the Indo-Americans.*

---

\* "On the following morning I saw an Indian corpse staged, or put upon a few cross sticks, about ten feet from the

3. The practice of *tattooing*, or imprinting indelible marks upon the skin,—a singular practice which appears to have prevailed at one time over all the islands of the Pacific, but of the origin of which no satisfactory account is given by the islanders themselves—is found also among certain of the native tribes of North America. It was observed, for instance, by Captain Vancouver among the Indians of Nootka Sound; and the Rev. Mr. West informs us, in his "Journal of a Residence in the Red River Colony," that it is occasionally observed among the Indians of Hudson's Bay. From a passage in the Book of Leviticus it would appear to have obtained among the ancient Egyptians, for we find a precept expressly prohibiting it in the Levitical law, conjoined with other precepts prohibiting other practices appa-

---

ground, at a short distance from the fort. The property of the dead, which may consist of a kettle, axe, and a few additional articles, is generally put into the case, or wrapped in the buffalo skin with the body, under the idea that the deceased will want them, or that the spirit of these articles will accompany the departed spirit in travelling to another world."—Journal of a Residence at the Red River Colony, British North America; by the Rev. John West, A.M.

rently indifferent; but which, it has been ascertained, were religious, or rather heathenish, observances of that ancient people. " Ye shall not eat anything with the blood: neither shall ye use enchantment, nor observe times. Ye shall not round the corners of your heads; neither shalt thou mar the corners of thy beard. Ye shall not make any cuttings in your flesh for the dead,* NOR PRINT ANY MARKS UPON YOU: I am the Lord." Levit. xix., 26, 28. On my second visit to New Zealand, in 1873, I had the honour of being introduced to a *Maori* chief, a member of the colonial Parliament, which was then in session in the city of Wellington, whose face was tattooed all over.

---

* *Cuttings for the dead* are also frequent in the South Sea Islands. On the occasion of my visit to the cemetery of the native village of Kororadika, in the Bay of Islands, in New Zealand, in 1839, the celebration of the anniversary of the death of a native chief who had died years before, and whose body had been wrapped up in native mats and deposited on the trestles, was held at the cemetery by a number of natives, both men and women. The body had been unwrapped from its casements, and the mere skeleton—all that remained—was exposed on the ground. Ever and anon unearthly howlings were uttered by both men and women, the latter cutting their faces with mussel shells till the blood flowed copiously down their cheeks.

4. I have already mentioned the horrible practice of the Polynesians of the olden time in Tahiti—that of *Tiputa Taata,* as they called it, or parading in triumph over a fallen enemy, with his body converted into a *poncho* for the victor.\* This is one of the last points of identification that one could have expected to realise among the Indo-Americans. And yet we do find it, as is evident from the following extract from Dr. Robertson's History of America. Speaking of warfare in Mexico, Dr. Robertson remarks:—"No captive was ever ransomed or spared. All were sacrificed without mercy, and their flesh devoured with as much barbarous joy as among the fiercest savages. On some occasions it rose to even wilder excesses. Their principal warriors covered themselves with the skins of the unhappy victims, and danced about the streets, boasting of their own valour, and exulting over their enemies.†"

5. The fifth and last of the proofs I shall offer of the identity of the Polynesian and Indo-Ameri-

---

\* Page 85.

† Robertson's History of America. Book VII., 226.

can races is the remarkable fact, to which I have already adverted at considerable length, of there being a language of deference or ceremony among the more developed groups of Polynesia, as there is among the Indo-Chinese nations of Asia and the Indian Archipelago.* For, strange and unaccountable as it may seem, the very same thing obtained in Mexico—there being there also, as in Polynesia, a language of deference and ceremony distinct from the language of common life.

"The distinction of ranks," says Dr. Robertson, "was completely established, in a regular line of subordination, reaching from the highest to the lowest members of the community. Each of these knew what he could claim, and what he owed. The people, who were not allowed to wear a dress of the same fashion, or to dwell in houses of a form similar to those of the nobles, accepted them with the utmost submissive reverence. In the presence of their sovereign, they durst not lift their eyes from the ground, or look him in the face. The nobles themselves, when admitted to

---

* Pages 51, 53.

an audience of their sovereign, entered barefoot, in mean garments, and, as his slaves, paid him homage approaching to adoration." This respect, due from inferiors to those above them in rank, was prescribed with such ceremonious accuracy that it incorporated with the language, and influenced its genius and idiom. The Mexican tongue abounded in expressions of reverence, and courtesy. The style and appellations used in the intercourse between equals would have been so unbecoming in the mouth of one in a lower sphere, when he accosted a person of higher rank, as to be deemed an insult. " The Mexicans had not only reverential nouns, but reverential verbs."*

In regard to the period in which America was originally discovered and settled by mankind, I am happy to find that the Honourable Albert Gallatin, LL.D., a distinguished Statesman, and one of the ablest philologists of North America, who has written very learnedly on the Indo-American tribes of the northern continent, and especially on their languages and migrations, is pre-

---

* Robertson's History of America. Book VII., p. 222.

cisely of the same opinion with myself not only as to the great antiquity of the Indo-American race, but also as to the period at which the easterly emigration commenced from the plain of Shinar, as well as to when that emigration may have reached America. Adopting the Hebrew chronology of Holy Scripture, as I have done, Mr. Gallatin thus writes :—

"Whilst the unity of structure and of grammatical forms proves a common origin, it may be inferred from this, combined with the great diversity and entire difference in the words of the several languages of America, that this continent received its first inhabitants at a very remote epoch, probably not much posterior to that of the dispersion of mankind." "After making every allowance, I cannot see any possible reason that should have prevented those who, after the dispersion of mankind, moved towards the east and north-east from having reached the extremities of Asia, and passed over to America, *within five hundred years after the flood*. However small may have been the number of those first emigrants, an equal number of years would have been more than sufficient to occupy in their own way every part of America."*

Mr. Gallatin doubtless conducts his first batch of emigrants to America by a somewhat different route from the one I have indicated in this volume, viz., by that well-known macadamised royal road from the Old World to America, that has been traversed in imagination by literary men of all classes and of all nations for three hundred years past. But whether he passes these emigrants across Behring's Straits, on the ice or in canoes, and how they happened to have left all their live stock behind them, the deponent saith not. I shall have something to say about the said Behring's Straits road to America in the sequel.

---

* A Synopsis of the Indian tribes within the United States east of the Rocky Mountains, and in the British and Russian possessions in North America. By the Hon. Albert Gallatin. Archaeologia Americana, vol. ii., Boston, 1836.

## CHAPTER VIII.

THERE IS NO EVIDENCE, AND NOT THE SLIGHTEST PROBABILITY, OF ANY EMIGRATION HAVING EVER TAKEN PLACE FROM ASIA TO AMERICA BY BEHRING'S STRAITS.

"THOUGH it be possible," observes Dr. Robertson, "that America may have received its first inhabitants from our continent, either by the north-west of Europe, or the north-east of Asia, there seems to be good reason for supposing that the progenitors of all the American nations, from Cape Horn to the southern confines of Labrador, migrated from the latter rather than the former. The Esquimaux are the only people in America, who, in their aspect or character, bear any resemblance to the northern Europeans. They are manifestly a race of men distinct from all the nations of the American continent, in language, in disposition, and in habits of life. Their original, then, may warrantably be traced up to that source which I have pointed out. But among all the other inhabitants of America there is such a striking similitude in the form of their bodies, and the qualities of their minds, that notwithstanding the diversities occasioned by the influence of climate, or unequal progress in improvement, we must pronounce them to be descended from one source. There may be a variety in the shades, but we can everywhere trace the same original colour. Each tribe has something peculiar which distinguishes it, but in all of them we discern certain features common to the whole race. It is remarkable, that in every peculiarity, whether in their persons or dispositions, which characterises the Americans, they have some resemblance to the rude tribes scattered over the north-east of Asia, but almost none to the nations settled in the northern extremities of Europe. We may therefore refer them to the former origin, and conclude that their Asiatic progenitors, having settled in those parts of America, where the Russians had discovered the proximity of the two continents, spread gradually over its various regions."*

---

* Robertson's History of America, Book V., page 90.

In this passage, Dr. Robertson lays down the three following points:—First, that the Esquimaux are the only aboriginal people in America entirely distinct from all the Indo-American tribes, and probably of European origin; secondly, that all the Indo-American tribes are one people, and sprung from the same source; and thirdly, that in all probability their progenitors arrived in America by Behring's Straits.

As we shall have but little occasion, in the sequel, to refer to the Esquimaux, we may dispose of what Dr. Robertson says of them at once. "They are of a middle size," that eminent historian adds, "and robust; with heads of a disproportioned bulk, and feet as remarkably small. Their complexions though swarthy, by being continually exposed to the rigour of a cold climate, inclines to the European white, rather than to the copper colour of America, and the men have beards, which are sometimes bushy and long. From these marks of distinction, as well as from one still less equivocal, the affinity of their language to that of the Greenlanders, we may conclude, with some degree of confidence, that the Esquimaux are a race different from the rest of the Americans."*

"As early as the ninth century (A.D. 830.)" Dr. Robertson continues, "the Norwegians discovered Greenland, and planted colonies there. The communication with that country, after a long interruption, was renewed in the seventeenth century. Some Lutheran and Moravian missionaries, prompted by zeal for propagating the Christian faith, ventured to settle in this frozen and uncultivated region. To them we are indebted for much curious information with respect to its nature and inhabitants. We learn that the north-west coast of Greenland is separated from America by a very narrow strait; that, at the bottom of the bay into which this strait conducts, it is highly probable that they are united; that the inhabitants of the two countries have some intercourse with one another; that the Esquimaux of America perfectly resemble the Greenlanders in their aspect, dress, and mode of

---

* Ibid, page 97.

living; that some sailors who had acquired the knowledge of a few words in the Greenlandish language, reported that these were understood by the Esquimaux; that, at length, (A.D. 1764) a Moravian missionary, well acquainted with the language of Greenland, having visited the country of the Esquimaux, found, to his astonishment, that they spoke the same language with the Greenlanders; that they were in every respect the same people, and he was accordingly received and entertained by them as a friend and a brother."*

The long interruption of all communication between Norway and Greenland, of which Dr. Robertson speaks, is supposed by some authorities to have arisen from an extraordinary irruption of icebergs from the north along the east coast of Greenland, thereby intensifying the rigour of the climate, and cutting off all communication with the mother country. It is alleged, however, by others that there had been a

---

\* Ibid, page 89. Dr. Robertson's informant was the Rev. Hans Egede, the zealous and devoted Moravian missionary of last century, in Greenland.

great sinking of the land along the east coast of Greenland; the houses of the old colonists being still visible in the deep water off the coast. At all events it is more than merely probable, and may be assumed as an ascertained fact, that certain of the Greenlanders had crossed over the narrow strait that separates Greenland from America, and there developed themselves in the course of ages into the people called the Esquimaux.

"Not having had access," observes Mr. Gallatin, in the Paper quoted above, " to Egede's Grammar and Dictionary of the Greenlandish language, a specimen only could be given, taken from his and from Crantz's accounts of Greenland. There is not, it is believed, any extant vocabulary of the Western Coast of Labrador. It differs so far from that of Greenland that the Moravian Missionaries were obliged to make a new translation of the Gospels for the use of the Labrador-Esquimaux, the one previously made for that of Greenland not being sufficiently intelligible to the other tribe. An examination of both has, however, enabled the learned authors of the 'Mithridates' to ascertain the great affinity of the two dialects, in reference both to words and to grammatical forms."*

It is not at all remarkable that the language of the Eastern Greenlanders should have become unintelligible to the Western, in the long series of ages that had elapsed from the discovery and settlement of Greenland by the Norwegians in the year 830, to the middle of the 18th century, when the Moravian Mission was established. How greatly has our own language changed in much less time than this! But it is very remarkable indeed that the Esquimaux, who thus represent the Greenlanders, should have occupied a narrow strip of land along the Polar circle in America, as Mr. Gallatin informs us they have actually done from the East Coast of Greenland to Behring's Straits —a distance of not less than five thousand four hundred miles, following the convolutions of the land—along the whole of which line the Esquimaux language prevails, and the Esquimaux people practice the same customs and wear the same sort of dress.

* Mr. Gallatin, *ubi supra*.

Nay, there is something more remarkable still in this Esquimaux case; for while there is no evidence of any North Asian tribe having ever crossed Behring's Straits into America, there is unquestionable evidence of the Esquimaux having found their way, somewhere near the Polar circle from America into Asia, in the existence of a small tribe called the Tchucktchi, on the northwestern shore of Behring's Straits, who speak the Esquimaux language, and practice the customs, and use the dress of the Esquimaux people. "They are as yet," says Mr. Gallatin, "The only well ascertained instance of an Asiatic tribe, belonging to the same race as any of the natives of North America."*

With the single exception, therefore, of the Esquimaux, Dr. Robertson regards the Indo-Americans as one people, sprung from the same source; and he further represents their forefathers as having reached America by Behring's Straits many ages ago. In short, it has been the general opinion of the learned for the last three hun-

---
* Gallatin, *ubi supra*,

dred years that America was originally peopled from North-eastern Asia, and, ever since the discovery of Behring's Straits, by that particular route: the great immigrations from which the Indo-Americans are supposed to be descended consisting of the Tartar hordes of North-eastern Asia, who had been defeated by Zenghis Khan in the thirteenth century, and had somehow found their way, in flying for some place of refuge from their ruthless conqueror, to America.

Now, it is somewhat remarkable, as an instance of the blindfold manner in which even the learned of all nations adopt conclusions in matters of importance, without either the slightest evidence or the slightest probability to support them, that ever since the first proposer of this particular route for the discovery and settlement of America announced his great idea to the world, the learned of all nations, including even such names as those of Humboldt and Dr. Robertson, have caught at and adopted that idea and followed in his wake—as blindly, indeed, and as unintelligently as a flock of sheep follows its leader.

In one word, Man's thoughts for three hundred years past, as to the discovery and peopling of America, have been that it must have taken place, at a comparatively recent period, from North-eastern Asia, by way of the farthest North, or Behring's Straits; but God's thoughts—discernible as they are very clearly from the event—were unquestionably that America should be discovered and settled in the infancy of our race by a party of Polynesians, whose forefathers had previously crossed the vast Pacific Ocean from the Indian Archipelago to Easter Island, and from thence to America.

" My thoughts are not your thoughts, neither are your ways My ways, saith the Lord. For as the heavens are higher than the earth, so are My ways higher than your ways, and My thoughts than your thoughts."* Now, there is perhaps no other instance in the history of mankind in which the thoughts, even of the wisest of men, have been more notably and more remarkably turned into folly than in this very case of the original disco-

---
* Isaiah lv. 8, 9.

very and progressive settlement of the Continent of America. "God Himself, that formed the earth and made it, He hath established it; He created it not in vain; He formed it to be inhabited."* Now, as the continents of Asia and America approach each other very closely in the far north, it was certainly the only natural inference imaginable by men of intelligence that certain of the inhabitants of the one continent should have passed over the narrow strait that divides them, to inhabit the other. And this has accordingly been man's thought on the subject these three centuries past. But God's thoughts—discoverable only, as I have already observed, from the event—was as different from all this as the heavens are from the earth. God's thought, I repeat it, was that America should be discovered and settled far south in the southern continent by a party of Polynesians, the descendants of men who had previously been driven by adverse westerly gales across the vast Pacific Ocean to the American land. Who could ever have imagined beforehand that such a course

---

* Isaiah xlv. 18.

should ever have been adopted, as we have seen it has, for the carrying out of the Divine purpose that America should be inhabited? And all the ridicule that has hitherto been thrown upon the idea—and there has been not a little since I first announced it, more than forty years since—by able editors and reviewers, only confirms the fact that God's thoughts in such matters are not our thoughts, nor His ways our ways.

There is nothing enthusiastic, there is nothing fanatical, as it will doubtless be alleged that there is, in this idea. It is simply the plain philosophical deduction from the reasoning I have adduced above, and the facts I have established.

For I maintain, without fear of contradiction, that there is neither the shadow of evidence nor the slightest probability of any emigration having ever taken place either on a small or on a large scale from north-eastern Asia to America by way of Behring's Straits.

First, then, as to the want of evidence. Had there ever been such an emigration, it would surely have left behind it some evidence of the fact in the existence of a third community in Aboriginal America, besides those of Indo-Americans on the one hand, and of Esquimaux on the other. We can easily account for the mere handful of Greenlanders who had crossed over the narrow strait that divides their country from America at some early period within the last thousand years, in the existence of the Esquimaux in America; but where is there any such evidence of any other emigration of any kind having taken place to America by Behring's Straits, or by any other conceivable land route? Supposing, therefore, for the moment, that there had been such an emigration to America, whether from Europe or Asia, it is evident that it must have perished on the spot, leaving no seed and no sign; for there is no such third aboriginal people in America, as in such a case there must have been. I shall be told, doubtless, that the emigrants from Asia generally, and particularly the large body of emigrants who are supposed to have fled from the conquering hosts of Zenghis Khan, were gradually amalgamated with the Indo-American nations, and ceased to maintain their separate national existence. But I reply, that it has never been either the policy or the practice of the Indo-Americans to amalgamate with people of a different race. Like the Jews, they have ever dwelt alone and been separate from the rest of the nations. And, consequently, as no such amalgamated communities have ever been discovered, there is reason to believe that none have ever existed.

There is a favourite idea on this subject that was long entertained, although now generally exploded, both in England and America, viz., that the Indians of America are the lineal descendants and representatives of the ten lost tribes of ancient Israel.

The principal advocates of this theory, which is supported only by feeble, fanciful, and far-fetched analogies, are Lord Kingsborough, a British peer, and a Dr. Boudinot, of America. Mr. Bancroft, of San Francisco, has, in his own learned work, given the following sketch of Lord Kingsborough and his writings on this subject :—

" Kingsborough has a theory to prove, and to accomplish his object he drafts every shadow of an analogy into his service. But though his theory is as wild as the wildest, and his proofs are as vague as the vaguest, yet Lord Kingsborough cannot be classed with such writers as Jones, Ranking, Cabrera, Adair, and the host of other dogmatists who have fought tooth and nail, each for his particular hobby. Kingsborough was an enthusiast, a fanatic if you choose— but his enthusiasm is never offensive. There is a scholarly dignity about his work which has never been attained by those who have jeered and railed at him; and though we may smile at his credulity, and regret that such strong zeal was so strangely misplaced, yet we should speak and think with respect of one who spent his lifetime and his fortune, if not his reason, in an honest endeavour to cast light upon one of the most obscure spots in the history of man."

The more prominent of the analogies adduced by Lord Kingsborough may be briefly enumerated as follows:—

"The religion of the Mexicans strongly resembled that of the Jews in many minor details, as will be presently seen, and the two were practically alike to a certain extent in their very foundation; for as the Jews acknowledged a multitude of angels, archangels, principalities, thrones, dominions, and powers, as the subordinate personages of their hierarchy, so did the Mexicans acknowledge the unity of the Deity in the person of Tezcatlipoca, and at the same time worship a great number of other imaginary beings. Both believed in a plurality of devils subordinate to one head, who was called by the Mexicans Mictlantliopochtli, and by the Jews Satan. Indeed, it seems that the Jews actually worshipped and made offerings to Satan, as the Mexicans did to their god of hell. It is probable that the Toltecs were acquainted with the sin of the first man, committed at the suggestion of the woman, herself deceived by the serpent, who tempted her with the fruit of the forbidden tree, who was the origin of all our calamities, and by whom death came into the world. We have seen in this chapter that Kingsborough supposes the Messiah and His story to have been familiar to the Mexicans."

"There is reason to believe that the Mexicans, like the Jews, offered meat and drink offerings to stones. There are striking similarities between the Babel, flood, and creation myths of the Hebrews and the Americans. Both Jews and Mexicans were fond of appealing in their adjurations to the heavens and the earth. Both were extremely superstitious, and firm believers in prodigies. The character and history of Christ and Huitzilopochtli present certain analogies. It is very probable that the Sabbath of the seventh day was known in some parts of America. The Mexicans applied the blood of sacrifices to the same uses as the Jews; they poured it upon the earth, they sprinkled it, they marked persons with it, and they smeared it upon walls and other inanimate things. No one but the Jewish High-priest might enter the Holy of Holies. A similar custom obtained in Peru. Both Mexicans and Jews regarded certain animals as unclean and unfit for food. Some of the Americans believed, with the Talmudists, in a plurality of souls. That man was created in the image of God was a part of the Mexican belief. It was customary among the Mexicans to eat the flesh of sacrifices of atonement. There are many points of resemblance between Tezcatlipoca and Jehovah. Ablutions formed an essential part of the ceremonial law of the Jews and Mexicans. The opinions of the Mexicans with regard to the resurrection of the body accorded with those of the Jews. The Mexican temple, like the Jewish, faced the east. 'As amongst the Jews the ark was a sort of portable temple, in which the Deity was supposed to be continually present, and which was accordingly borne on the shoulders of the priests, as a sure refuge and defence from their enemies, so amongst the Mexicans and the Indians of Michoacan and Honduras an ark was held in the highest veneration, and was considered an object too sacred to be touched by any but the priests. The same religious reverence for the ark is stated by Adair to have existed among the Cherokee and other Indian tribes inhabiting the banks of the Mississippi; and his testimony is corroborated by the accounts of Spanish authors of the greatest veracity. The nature and use of the ark having been explained, it is needless to observe that its form might have been various, although Scripture declares that the Hebrew ark was of the simplest construction.'" And again. "It would appear from many passages of the Old Testament that the Jews believed in the real presence of God in the ark, as the Roman Catholics believe in the real presence of Christ in the sacrament, from whom it is probable the Mexicans borrowed the notion that He, whom the heaven of heavens cannot contain, and whose glory fills all space, could be confined within the precincts of a narrow ark, and be borne by a set of weak and frail priests. If the belief of the Mexicans had not been analogous to that of the ancient Jews, the early Spanish missionaries would certainly have expressed their indignation at the absurd credulity of those who believed that their omnipresent god, Huitzilopochtli, was carried in an ark on priests' shoulders; but of the ark of the Mexicans they say but little, fearing, as it would appear, to tread too boldly on the burning ashes of Mount Sinai."

"The Yucatec conception of a Trinity resembles the Hebrew. It is probable that Quetzalcoatl, whose proper name signifies, "feathered serpent," was so called after the brazen serpent which Moses lifted up in the Wilderness; the feathers, perhaps, alluding to the Rabbinical tradition that the fiery serpents which God sent against the Israelites were of a winged species."*

After the specimen we have just had of Lord Kingsborough's zealous but futile efforts to identify the Indo-Americans with the Ten Lost Tribes of Ancient Israel, the reader will doubtless think, with Mr. Bancroft, that we have had quite enough of his Lordship's "unreadable book!"

The following account of the opinions entertained on the subject, of the alleged identity of the Indo-Americans and the Lost Ten Tribes of

---

*"The Native Races of the Pacific States of North America." By Hubert Howe Bancroft, vol. v. London—Pages 84 to 87.

Israel, by the learned in America, and especially by an eminent American advocate of that hypothesis, Dr. Elias Boudinot, is taken from the *Princeton Review*, a very able and influential American journal, for the month of January, 1841, thirty-five years ago :—

" We have yet said nothing of a theory widely circulated in this country, and embracing among its advocates some very distinguished men. We refer to the opinion that the Indians of North America, at least, are the descendants of Abraham, and a portion of the long lost ten tribes carried away from the land of Israel by the King of Assyria, and their place filled up by other people sent to take their place. This event, according to Ussher's chronology, occurred about 720 years before the Christian era. (See 2 Kings, xvii.) That which invests this opinion—otherwise very improbable—with some plausibility and interest, is, that most of those who have been its advocates have either resided among the American Indians, or have received their information from those who had lived among them, and were well acquainted with their customs and religious ceremonies."

"A distinguished statesman and philanthropist of our own country, Elias Boudinot, LLD., has entered zealously into the defence of this opinion, in a work entitled 'The Star in the West,' which, when first published, attracted considerable attention, and probably made some converts to the opinion of the learned author. As the work is readily accessible to any one who desires to peruse it, we decline entering into any detail respecting the arguments and facts depended on to sustain the hypothesis. Both of these authors refer the emigration to a period when the first temple was yet standing, when Shalmaneser carried captive the ten tribes, as before mentioned. This theory does not propose a new method of reaching the American continent, but takes it for granted that the emigrants passed into America from the northeast of Asia. Our reasons for dissenting from this opinion are, that the aborigines of America have not the obscurest tradition of any such descent, or of any of the remarkable facts recorded in the Mosaic history, which could no more have been utterly lost than their language; and this again furnishes another strong argument against the hypothesis in question; for, as far as we know, it has never been alleged by any Hebraist that the languages of our Indian tribes have any affinity, or the least resemblance to the ancient Hebrew. We have, indeed, seen a collection of words from the language of the Carribees, which had a resemblance to Hebrew words of the same signification: but the hypothesis under consideration relates to our wandering tribes in North America, from whose religious ceremonies all the arguments are derived. But the entire diversity of languages among these tribes, already mentioned, is inconsistent with the idea that, originally, they all used one tongue; for, living in the same country, such an entire diversity could never have occurred; but the most conclusive argument is the universal defect of the covenant seal of circumcision, by which all the descendants of Abraham, in every line, are distinguished, and which is of itself sufficient to overthrow the theory;

and as to the arguments derived from certain religious observances and ceremonies, they are such as that something similar may be found in many nations who certainly cannot claim any kindred with Abraham. This similarity of religious rites among different nations rather goes to prove that the religions of the heathen nations had a common origin, and that they were derived from institutions of divine appointment, which, however, were greatly perverted from their original design.

"That remarkable man, Joseph Wolf, has spent many years in travelling over the earth, to see if he could find the habitation of the Ten Tribes; and with the view, it is said, of ascertaining whether there was any foundation for the opinion which we have been considering, came to this country, intending to visit the several tribes in the United States; but, when he was at Washington city, he had the opportunity of seeing a number of Indian chiefs, from several tribes, and whether from these specimens he was satisfied that they had no claim to be considered the seed of Abraham, or whether other reasons induced him to decline, we cannot tell, but he relinquished his purpose of going among the Indian tribes, and, we have understood, had no belief that they had any connexion with the tribes of Israel. And, although on many subjects we should be unwilling to confide in the judgment of this benevolent enthusiast, yet, in regard to this point, we know no one whose opinion should be more decisive, especially when it is found on the negative of the question."

There is one remarkable peculiarity characteristic of the Indo-Americans in all parts of that continent, and in all climates, that precludes the possibility of their having originated in any other than one source—the Indo-Americans, therefore, are all red, or, rather brown men. On this point the very able American journal from which I have just been quoting a long extract, makes the following observations:—

" There is only one circumstance in the case of the aborigines of America which seems to have no analogy to the other nations of the earth, and that is the uniformity of their complexion, from Labrador to Cape Horn. We confess that, considering the many climates which they occupy, it seems somewhat unaccountable that there should be such a uniformity of colour. The Spanish writers who gave an account of the first discovery of America, mention this fact with great surprise. They expected to find the inhabitants of the countries within the tropics of as dark a colour as in Asia or Africa, but they found little or no change of complexion from that of the higher latitudes."

I have stated above that there is not only no evidence, but not the slightest probability of any emigration having ever taken place from northeastern Asia to America, by Behring's Straits; and I now proceed to state my reasons for holding this opinion.

"The actual vicinity of the two continents is," says Dr. Robertson, "so clearly established by modern discoveries that the chief difficulty with respect to the peopling of America is removed. While those immense regions which stretch eastward from the river Oby to the sea of Kamtschatka were unknown or imperfectly explored, the north-east extremities of our hemisphere were supposed to be so far distant from any part of the New World that it was not easy to conceive how any communication should have been carried on between them; but the Russians, having subjected the western part of Siberia to their empire, gradually extended their knowledge of that vast country by advancing towards the east into unknown provinces. These were discovered by hunters in their excursions after game, or by soldiers employed in levying the taxes; and the Court of Moscow estimated the importance of those countries only by the small addition which they made to its revenue. At length Peter the Great ascended the Russian throne; his enlightened, comprehensive mind, intent upon every circumstance that could aggrandize his empire, or render his reign illustrious, discerned consequences of those discoveries which had escaped the observation of his ignorant predecessors; he perceived that, in proportion as the regions of Asia extended towards the east, they must approach nearer to America; that the communication between the two continents, which had long been searched for in vain, would probably be found in this quarter; and that, by opening it, some part of the wealth and commerce of the western world might be made to flow into his dominions by a new channel. Such an object suited a genius that delighted in grand schemes. Peter drew up instructions with his own hand for prosecuting this design, and gave orders for carrying it into execution."*

The following is a copy of the Instructions which the Czar, Peter the Great, left for his successors on the throne of Russia, for the discovery of America from the west.

### 1728.

"1. You shall cause one or two convenient vessels to be built at Kamtschatka, or elsewhere; 2. You shall endeavour to discover, by coasting with these vessels, whether the country towards the north, of which we have no distinct knowledge, is a part of America or not; 3. If it joins

---

* Robertson, Book IV., 87.

the continent of America, you shall endeavour, if possible, to reach some colony belonging to some European power; or, in case you meet with any European ship, you shall diligently enquire the name of the coasts, and such other circumstances as it is in your power to learn, and these you shall commit to writing, so that we may have some certain memoirs by which a chart may be constructed."*

Peter's instructions were, in due time, carried into effect by his successors, and especially by the famous Russian Empress Catherine; for, in 1741—

" Orders were issued to build two vessels at the small village of Ochotz, situated on the sea of Kamtschatka, to sail on a voyage of discovery. Though that dreary uncultivated region furnished nothing that could be of use in constructing them, but some larch trees; though not only the iron, the cordage, the sails, and all the numerous articles requisite for their equipment, but the

---

\* Account of the Russian Discoveries between Asia and America. By William Coxe, A.M., London, 1803.

provisions for victualling them, were to be carried through the immense deserts of Siberia, down rivers of difficult navigation, and along roads almost impassable, the mandate of the sovereign, and the perseverance of the people, at last surmounted every obstacle. Two vessels were finished, and, under the command of the captains Behring and Tschirikow, sailed from Kamtschatka, in quest of the New World, in a quarter where it had never been approached. They shaped their course towards the east; and though a storm soon separated the vessels, which never rejoined, and many disasters befel them, the expectations from the voyage were not altogether frustrated. Each of the commanders discovered land, which to them appeared to be part of the American continent."*

Though the islands (discovered by Behring and Tschirikow) were frequented from that time by Russian hunters, the Court of St. Petersburgh, during a period of more than thirty years, seems to have relinquished every thought of prosecuting discoveries in that quarter. "But, in the year

---

* Robertson, Book IV., page 88.

1768 it was unexpectedly resumed. The sovereign who had then been lately seated on the throne of Peter the Great, possessed the genius and talents of her illustrious predecessor. During the operations of the most arduous and extensive war in which the Russian empire was ever engaged, she formed schemes and executed undertakings to which more limited abilities would have been incapable of attending, but amidst the leisure of pacific times. A new voyage of discovery from the eastern extremity of Asia was planned, and Captain Krenitzin and Lieutenant Levasheff were appointed to command the two vessels fitted out for that purpose. In their voyage outward they held nearly the same course with the former navigators, they touched at the same islands, observed their situation and productions more carefully, and discovered several new islands, with which Behring and Tschirikow had not fallen in. Though they did not proceed so far to the east as to revisit the country which Behring and Tschirikow supposed to be part of the American continent, yet, by returning in a course considerably to the north of theirs, they corrected some capital mistakes into which their predecessors had fallen, and have contributed to facilitate the progress of future navigators in those seas."*

It was, therefore, Captain Vitus Behring, a German officer in the Russian naval service, who discovered the strait that bears his name, and that divides the continent of Asia from America, in the year 1741. "When Behring discovered America," says a recent American traveller, "he sailed a short distance along its coast, and then steered for Kamtschatka. The commander was confined to his cabin by illness, and the crew suffered severely from scurvy. 'At one period,' says Steller, the historian of the voyage, 'only ten persons were capable of duty, and they were too weak to furl the sails, so that the ship was left to the elements. Not only the sick died, but those who pretended to be healthy fainted and fell down dead when relieved from their posts. In this condition the navigators were drifted upon

* Robertson, *ubi supra.*

a rocky island, where their ship went to pieces, but not until all had landed. Many of the crew died soon after going on shore; but the transfer from the ship appeared to diminish the ravages of the scurvy. Captain Behring died on the eighth of December, and was buried in the trench where he lay. The island where he perished bears his name, but his grave is unmarked. An iron monument to his memory was recently erected at Petropaulovsk."*

And yet the perilous navigation of this Strait of Behring, which was fraught with so much hardship, suffering, and death to its first discoverers—although all the while in ships of war, and possessed of all the appliances of modern navigation, including plenty of provisions—is regarded by the able editors and reviewers who sit and write their imaginary histories in their warm parlours in London, as plain and simple a process as the crossing of the British Channel; insomuch that even the rude, poverty-stricken

---

* Overland through Asia: Pictures of Siberian, Chinese, and Tartar Life. By Thomas W. Knox. London, 1871., page 65.

savages of Kamtschatka are supposed to be quite able to cross the strait between Asia and America in their skin coracles, and as easily as a waterman of our time can pass from Dover to Calais. Nay, so plain and simple does the passage seem to these authorities, that myriads of Tartars, flying after their defeat from the ruthless conqueror Zenghis Khan, are supposed to have been able to find their way across it, after a long previous journey of four or five thousand miles on land, and without compass, without chart, and without provisions of any kind—and yet this is the general creed on the subject! Surely credulity can no farther go!

At its narrowest point, in latitude 66° N., Behring's Strait is only about forty-seven miles wide; but as the aborigines of that part of the Asiatic continent (who must originally have reached their actual settlements overland from Siberia, and who belong to a tribe called *Tchuktchis*) are in the lowest state of social debasement, we cannot surely give them the credit of at once transforming themselves into able mariners, and crossing the strait, for no object whatever, to America. They could never have known of the existence of that continent till its discovery by Captain Behring; and it is altogether out of the question to suppose that they could have gone in search of it. For my own part—from what I know of sea life—I cannot believe that Behring's Strait was ever crossed by mortal man till after its discovery by Captain Behring.

But the grand event to which, it seems, we are to look for the peopling of America in past ages is the defeat of a large host of his enemies by the great Tartar conqueror, Zenghis Khan, somewhere in Central Asia, and the flight of the vanquished in one vast body to some place of safety and of settlement from the ruthless conqueror. For it is alleged that the vanquished myriads on that occasion crossed over the intervening tract of country to the north-eastern extremity of Asia, and from thence across Behring's Strait to America.

Zenghis Khan was born in the year 1160, and died in 1227. Now, supposing for the moment that the supposition of that vast emigration of thousands and tens of thousands of his vanquished enemies from Central Asia to America is well founded, it must have occurred in the first place at least two hundred and fifty years before America was discovered; that great achievement of Columbus having taken place in the year 1492, in the case of St. Domingo, and in 1498, in that of the mainland of America.

Again, supposing that the alleged emigration to America did take place, it must have been either from Bochara, one of Zenghis Khan's centres of movement, or from Pekin in China; for the great Tartar conqueror had great battles at both places. In the one case, the distance to be travelled over would have exceeded four thousand miles, and in the other it would have exceeded two. Besides, how were provisions to be found for the mighty host in the frightful Siberian deserts of which Robertson speaks in a passage already quoted? Finally, where were they to find shipping to carry them across to America when they had actually reached the farthest east in Asia? In one word, of all the schemes for the discovery and settlement of America that have been suggested at various times, and by different persons, there is none so pre-eminently absurd as the one that refers the peopling of America to the emigration of a host of the vanquished foes of the great Tartar, Zenghis Khan. I maintain therefore, without the slightest fear of contradiction, that there never has been, either on a large or on a small scale, any emigration from north-eastern Asia to America.

## CHAPTER IX.

### THERE IS NO VALID OBJECTION AGAINST THE THEORY OF THIS WORK FROM THE PHENOMENA OF LANGUAGE IN AMERICA.

It is a frequently expressed and seemingly reasonable idea that the aborigines of America must have been derived from various independent sources, and that those of the northern continent especially could not have had the same origin with those of the southern. The phenomena of language in America have often been triumphantly appealed to in support of this conclusion; for the languages of the two American continents are remarkably different from each other in their general aspect and character, and that of Mexico in particular from that of Peru.

Without entering for the present into the question as to whether the languages of North America could ever have originated in the same common source with those of the southern continent, I would simply ask, How the multifarious languages of the other three grand divisions of the habitable world were originated? Surely there are as great differences in the languages of Europe, Asia, and Africa respectively as there are in those of North and South America: and yet we have no hesitation in admitting that the multitude of tongues that are spoken in the three continents of the old world either originated with those eight persons who survived the deluge, or are traceable directly to that source. The question, therefore, resolves itself into a sort of rule-of-three question after all. For if the eight persons who survived the deluge originated all the languages that are spoken in all the three continents of the old world, how many might not other eight persons, supposing there were no more, who landed at Copiapo, in South America, in the infancy of our race, have originated, in much about the same period, in the new world? In short, if there are difficulties in the one case, there are difficulties equally great in the other: and I am not called on to show how the multitude of languages came to be developed from one common source in either case. The fact is obvious that it was so, but how it came to be so we cannot tell.

I cannot, therefore, admit for the reasons given at length in the previous chapters of this work, that the Indo-Americans have been derived from a variety of sources. On the contrary, I hold with those great men, Humboldt, Blumenbach, Robertson, the historian, Von Martius, of Bavaria, and Dr. Morton, of Philadelphia, that the Indo-Americans are all one people, of one origin, and derived from one common stock. And I hold also that in that one stock all the languages of both continents of America, how diverse soever from each other, originated.

After these preliminary observations, I now proceed to show that there is nothing in the phenomena of language in America to militate against the theory I have submitted in this work to all who feel interested in the subject, viz., that the Indo-Americans are of Polynesian origin, and that the forefathers of their nation consisted of a mere handful of South Sea Islanders, who, with their descendants in successive generations, had been driven by violent westerly gales from their native island in the Indian Archipelago, across the vast Pacific Ocean, first to Easter Island, near the American land, and from thence to some where near Copiapo in South America.

Taking it for granted then, for the moment, that this was the point of disembarkation for the forefathers of the Indo-American nation from their long voyages, or rather series of voyages, across the Pacific Ocean, it stands to reason that their descendants, in migrating to the northwards, as they certainly would along the slope of the Cordilleras, would leave behind them evidences of their language, as well as of their manners and customs, and especially of their architecture, in the regions through which they passed successively. Humboldt raises this probability to a certainty in the passage quoted above, in which he tells us that the only places in America in which the aborigines were gathered into large communities at the era of the Spanish conquest, were the western slope of the Cordilleras and the coast towards Asia; this remarkable testimony being confirmed by the fact which I have already mentioned, that along the royal highway of fifteen hundred miles which the Incas of Peru had formed between the royal cities of Cuzco and Quito, they had erected store houses for provisions at every ten or twelve miles, which they designated by the Polynesian name for such buildings Taboo, or (Tambo, as the Spaniards pronounced the word) meaning that these buildings were consecrated for a particular purpose by the sanctions of religion.

On one of my voyages to England, I happened to meet in London with a highly intelligent gentleman who had just then returned from British Guiana and the Demerara River, where he had been residing for a series of years. Desirous as I was at the time of ascertaining how far north the influence of the Polynesian character of the South American dialects might be felt, I requested the gentleman I allude to to give me a few specimens of words of the language of the

Indo-Americans in the interior of that colony, as also a few names of places and objects on the Demerara River. The following, therefore, is a specimen of the language of the Warows, an Indo-American tribe of British Guiana, which I am confident the intelligent reader will admit bears a striking resemblance to the language of Polynesia. Like that language, the language of the Indians of Guiana is essentially vocalic; that is, it abounds in vowel sounds, while every word terminates with a vowel. The same guttural aspirations, indicating the suppression of consonantal sounds, appear to prevail, as in the dialect of Tahiti; the same nasal sound occurs as in that of New Zealand; and in the formation of compound words, or the embodying of complex ideas, the same mental process that characterises the languages of the Indian Archipelago and of China is strikingly exhibited. In short, a scholar, whose eye and ear had been accustomed to trace the affinities or to detect the radical dissimilarity of different languages, would at once unhesitatingly assert that the following words of the dialect of the Warows of British Guiana were just so many words of the Polynesian tongue :—

| | |
|---|---|
| Head | Maquah. |
| Eyes | Maamu. |
| Mouth | Maroho. |
| Hair | Maaheo. |
| Ears | Mahohoko. |
| Arms | Mahaara. |
| Skin | Mahoro.* |

\* I apprehend the commencing syllable in all these words is merely a prefix. The same prefix occurs in the composition of many New Zealand words of exactly similar external appearance; as, for instance,

| | |
|---|---|
| Mahana | Day. |
| Marama | The Moon. |
| Maripi | A sword. |
| Madino | Smooth. |
| Maha | Much. |
| Matapo | Blind. |
| Blood | Hotuh. |
| Water | Ho. |
| Earth | Hotah. |

I apprehend the first syllable in the New Zealand words, *Hotuh* and *Hotah*, is the Polynesian article *e*, which in the New Zealand dialect is generally aspirated. *Hotuh* resembles the Tahitian word *to-to*, also signifying *blood;* and *hotah* is probably the remains of the Malayan word *tanah*, signifying land or country, with the Polynesian aspirated article.

| | |
|---|---|
| Sun | Yah.† |
| Moon | Waanehah. |
| Stars | Keorah. |
| Thunder | Nahaa. |
| Rain | Naahaa. |
| Paddle | Haabah. |
| Tobacco | Aoha. |

Examples of compound words.

| | |
|---|---|
| Grandmother | Naatu. |
| Grandchild | Naatusenga. |
| Hands | Yenarry. |
| Hand-appendages. (fingers) | Yenarry eteedeh. |
| Arrow | Semaara. |
| Arrow-discharger (bow) | Semaara haaba. |
| Arrow discharger-cord (bow-string) | Semaara haaba teemy. |

The following Indian names on the Demerara River very evidently also exhibit a Polynesian aspect : viz. Arigaraboe, Ioerawea, Hiagua, Haboe, Boera-boera-wa, Wara-warau, Maraka, Mamua, Moenetari, Mari-mari, Winipio, Mamikoeroa, Toematamatia, Motoka, Akyma, Kaiwalia, Kamakaiaha, Dalawila.

---

† The Polynesian word for *the sun* is *ra* or *la*; and it is quite accordant with the genius of that language for the semivowel ta be completely liquified, as in the Indo-American word *yah*.

The Indian names of several of the creeks or tributary streams that empty themselves into the Demerara River commence with the syllable *wa*, as Waridu, Waratili, Walaba. Wai or Vai is the Polynesian word for *water*.

Akuri, Marudi. Himara, Koekeruni, Tibikuri. are Indian words descriptive of objects of natural history in British Guiana. They exhibit the same Polynesian character and aspect.

Bauia, Kokarelli, Kabakali, Kanunubali, Karahuri, Kutabali, Dukali, Dukalibali, Gomaro, Hiabali, Hakia, Itikiburabali, Kurara, Kurakurara, Mora, Simarupa, Siwaro, Turaneara, Tataba, Wamara, Wadaduri, Yerura, Yurabali, are the Indian names of various species of forest-trees in British Guiana, with which I have also been favoured through the kindness of the friend already alluded to.

Many of the names of places in the equatorial regions of America are decidedly Polynesian in their sound and appearance. Of this description are such words as Peru. Quito (Kito), Guatimala (Katimala), Arica. Loa. Titicaca, Panama, Huayna,

Chili, Caicara, Atahualpa, Tiahuanacu, Arequipa (Arekipa), Guarohiri (Karohiri), Huanuco, Lima, Tarapaca, Guanaxato (Kanahato), Guanahani (Kanahani), the island first discovered by Columbus, Cuba, Huarina, Guacanahari (Kakanahari), Anacoana, Hatuey (a Haitian Chief), probably Ka Tooi.

One of the two numerals that Baron Humboldt gives in a list of words of the Chayma and Tamanack languages of Central America is *oroz* or *orua*, two. In all probability it is merely the Polynesian *dua* or *rua* with the Tahitian prefix or article.

The Mexican reverential affix, *tzin* or *azin*, which was always added to the names of princes, is in all likelihood the Rukheng or Indo-Chinese affix, *asyang*, signifying *lord*, if not the Chinese word *tsin*. In the list of Mexican kings who reigned previous to the era of the Spanish conquest, we find the names of Nopal-tzin, Ho-tzin, Quina-tzin (Kina-tzin), Cacama-tzin, Cuicuitzca-tzin, Coanaco-tzin, Montezuma-tzin, Guatimo-tzin (Ka-Tima-tzin). Several of these proper names have a remarkable resemblance to modern Polynesian names; the last, especially—the name of the unfortunate prince whom the Spaniards extended over a fire of coals to compel him to inform them where he had hidden his treasures—is, when stripped of its Spanish doublet and its reverential affix, a pure New Zealand name.

British Guiana is in latitude 6° 58' N., but there is another Indo-American language, called the Cora, which is spoken at the isthmus of Darien, in latitude 9° N., and which exhibits a still more striking resemblance to the Polynesian dialects, although I have unfortunately mislaid the specimens of it which I had copied out some years since. It is quite evident, therefore, that the vocalic character of the Polynesian languages has influenced and left its mark upon the Indo-American languages as far north as the ninth degree of north latitude.

The languages of South America have undoubtedly a much closer resemblance to the Polynesian dialects than those of the northern continent. It was evidently, however, by a race that spoke a language bearing a much closer resemblance to the Polynesian tongue than the present language of Mexico, that the largest and the most ancient of the pyramids of that country was erected—at least if we may judge from its decidedly Polynesian name, *Teotihuacan*, which is evidently a word of a very different family from such modern Mexican words as *Huitzilopochtli*, the god of war, and *Mictlancihuatl*, the goddess of hell. The Aztecks, or modern Mexicans, who had overrun the Mexican territory from the northward, and whose tenth king was the reigning monarch at the era of the Spanish invasion, ascribed the erection of the pyramid to the Toltecks, a tribe of kindred origin and language, who had also overrun Mexico five hundred years previous to the era of the Azteck conquest; but they did so simply because their chronology, which, like that of many other conquering tribes, overlooked the records and traditions of the vanquished people, did not extend any higher than the era of the emigration and conquests of the northern tribes. But the probability is that the pyramid of Teotihuacan was erected long before the Toltecks had emerged from the forests of the north, and that that warlike but less polished race retained the ancient Polynesian name of the stupendous edifice, while they worshipped their own national divinities, within its sacred precincts, under their own northern appellations. In short, the Mexican language, in all probability, received its birth in the forests of the northern continent, to which numerous tribes had doubtless emigrated from the southward many ages before the Azteck conquest of Mexico or the reflux of the northern tribes on the countries to the southward.

Humboldt seems to have been of a somewhat similar opinion himself, when he writes as follows in regard to the multiplicity of languages that were spoken in the northern continent:—

"The number of languages which distinguish the different native tribes appears still more considerable in the New Continent than in Africa, where, according to the late researches of Messrs. Seetzen and Vater, there are above one hundred and forty. In this respect the whole of America resembles Caucasus, Italy before the conquest of the Romans, Asia Minor when that country contained on a small extent of territory the Cilicians of Semitic race, the Phrygians of Thracian origin, the Lydians, and the Celts. The configuration of the soil, the strength of vegetation, the apprehensions of the mountaineers under the tropics of exposing themselves to the burning heat of the plains, are obstacles to communication, and contribute to the amazing variety of American dialects. This variety, it is observed, is more restrained in the savannahs and forests of the north, which are easily traversed by the hunter, on the banks of great rivers, along the coast of the ocean, and in every country where the Incas had established their theocracy by the force of arms."\*

Humboldt's assertion, however, that "the civilization of Mexico emanated from a country situated towards the north," is doubtless, in accordance with his preconceived opinion that America was originally peopled from the continent of Asia, across Behring's Straits; but, as that opinion is at least

---
\* Humboldt's Researches, vol. i., p. 17.

extremely problematical, the assertion is altogether gratuitous. It is much more probable that Mexico itself was the centre, or starting-point, of the more recent American civilization; from whence, in successive ages, the stream continued to flow both northward and southward, although a portion of that stream may in still later ages have returned again in the shape of a comparatively civilized and conquering tribe upon the Mexican territory. When Humboldt asserts, however, that " the problem of the first population of America is no more the province of history, than the question on the origin of plants and animals, and on the distribution of organic germs, are that of natural science," he merely cuts the knot which he is unable to untie. " It has hitherto been impossible," adds the accomplished traveller, " to ascertain the period when the communication between the inhabitants of the two worlds took place." I have attempted however to ascertain that period—with what success the reader will determine. " How rash," continues the Baron, " would be the attempt to point out the group of nations of the Old Continent, with which the Toltecks, the Aztecks, the Muyscas, and the Peruvians present the nearest analogies; since these analogies are apparent in the traditions, the monuments, and customs, which, perhaps, preceded the present division of Asiatics into Chinese, Moguls, Hindoos, and Tungooses."*

I have nevertheless made this attempt, and have shown that, independently of those more remote analogies to which the learned traveller alludes, there are other and far closer analogies subsisting between the Indo-Americans and the race that inhabits the South Sea Islands, and demonstrating that America was originally peopled across the broadest part of the vast Pacific Ocean by individuals of that ancient Asiatic and primitive race. Whether the attempt may have been characterised by *rashness*, or attended with success, it is for others to decide.

In a passage quoted above, Humboldt admits that the Aztecks, who had held the empire of Mexico for five hundred years previous to the Spanish conquest, referred the construction of the

---

* Humboldt's Researches, vol. i., p. 25.

pyramids of that country to the Toltecks, another Indo-American nation, who had previously held the country for other five hundred years merely as representing the highest antiquity they could conceive of. But there is reason to believe that both the pyramids of Peru—Teotihuacan on Lake Titicaca—and those of Mexico, described by the learned Baron, had been in ruins for at least a thousand years before either Aztecks or Toltecks were heard of in America. The earliest emigration of the Indo-American race, from their first settlement in South America, was necessarily, as I have shown above, along the western slopes of the Andes; and the pyramidal and colossal buildings, both of Mexico and Peru, are undoubtedly referable only to the men of that original emigration. I am happy to be confirmed in this opinion, as well as in the strictures I have just taken the liberty to pass on certain assertions of Humboldt, by the observations of a recent and accomplished traveller in Peru. The gentleman I refer to is E. G. Squier, Esq., M.A., Fellow of the Society of Antiquaries of London, whose paper, which is contained in the "American Naturalist," vol. iv. 1870, as also in "The Academy" of June 1st, 1871, is entitled *The Primæval Monuments of Peru compared with those in other parts of the world.*

Having quoted so largely from Humboldt's description of the pyramids of Mexico, I would limit my quotations from Mr. Squier to his observations on another form of Peruvian antiquities, viz., the Chulpas or burying places and mummy pits of that country.

The monuments Mr. Squier describes form a somewhat conspicuous part in Peruvian landscapes, since their height varies from one to forty feet above the ground; but the various travellers who have visited Peru since Pizarro's days did not care to enquire into the motives of their construction. This Mr. Squier has done, and, by comparing their style and character with those of the stone structures in the Old World, he has discovered that they belong to the early monumental period of American history, and that they are the exact counterparts of the so-called cromlechs, dolmens, "Tini," or Druidical circles of West Europe and Central Asia.

The simplest and most numerous of these monuments are, of course, the *chulpas*, in which the Andean tribes of yore buried their dead. There are, according to Mr. Squier's statement, several sorts of *chulpas*.

1. The first kind consists of flat unhewn stones, projecting from one to two feet above the ground, so as to form a circle about three feet in diameter. The inner space sometimes remains uncovered, and sometimes is roofed by a few flat slabs laid across the upright ones.

2. The stones rise from four to six feet above the ground; the diameter of the circle varies from six to sixteen feet. The upper stories, instead of lying flat across the upright ones, overlap each other inwardly, thus describing a kind of primitive vault. The entrance is provided for by omitting one of the upright stones.

3. Around the burial chamber a tower is built, varying in height from ten to thirty feet. The tower walls are often narrower at their base than

at their summit. The exterior stones are usually broken to conform to the outer curve of the tower, and the whole is more or less cemented together with a very tenacious clay.

4. The towers, raised or square, are built of square blocks of limestone, and stand on a platform regularly shaped; the inner parts, vaulted after the manner described in No. 2, have each four niches, placed at right angles to each other. The sides of the *chulpas*, whether round or square, are perfectly vertical, and have a projecting cornice near the summit. In the square ones the top is flat, and in the round ones there is a sort of rude cupola.

5. The towers are built of great blocks of trachyte, and other hard stones, accurately fitted together. A few are formed of rough stones, plastered and stuccoed, and painted all over, with inner chambers also painted and stuccoed. Some have double vaults in them, one above the other; the single vaulted ones have a double row of mitres in a single chamber.

Mr. Squier inclines to the opinion that these

various forms of the *chulpa* point to different eras. . . . "The *chulpa* probably marks the graves of distinguished individuals upon which contemporaneous skill and effort were expended."

. . . . "I am convinced, speaking for the present only of sepulchral monuments, that their development in Peru may be traced from their first and modest form up to that which prevailed at the time of the Conquest, and that it preserved, throughout, the same essential features."

Side by side with the *chulpas*, we find remains of religious monuments which have also escaped the notice of travellers: the *intihuatanas*, or *sun-circles*, stretch in many places their long lines, defined by rude upright stones, and surrounding one or more larger upright stones, placed sometimes in the centre of the circle, but oftener at one third of the diameter of the circle, apart, and on a line at right angles to another line through the centre of the gateway or entrance on the east. I have seen such a circle myself in the Orkney Islands, in Scotland. They are there called Druidical circles. From this, and the examination of the *Pucaras,* or Pre-Incassic strongholds, Mr. Squier feels justified in inferring that "there exists in Peru and Bolivia, high up among the snowy Andes, the oldest forms of sepulchral monuments known to mankind, exact counterparts, in character, of those of the old world, pervaded by a common design, and illustrating similar conceptions. All of these are the work of the same peoples found in occupation of the country at the time of the Conquest, whose later monuments are mainly, if not wholly, the developed forms of those raised by their ancestors; they seem to have been the spontaneous productions of the primitive man in all parts of the world, and they are not, necessarily, nor even probably, derivative.

The conclusion to which Mr. Squier was thus led from his personal examination of the sepulchral monuments and mummy pits of Peru was, that the erection of these structures was referable only to the highest antiquity, and that the people who erected them derived their knowledge and skill from the same common source as the other most ancient nations on the face of the earth.

In regard to the period at which the continent of America was originally discovered by some heaven-directed wanderers of the Polynesian nation, it is evident that a long series of ages must have rolled over the heads of its aboriginal nations ere such a state of things as America exhibited at the era of the Spanish conquest, in regard to the wide dispersion of its Indian population, could possibly have been arrived at. It follows, therefore, that even on this ground alone, independently of every other consideration, we must utterly reject the crude and irrational hypotheses of those fanciful philosophers who derive the Indo-American race either from a colony of shipwrecked Britons of the tenth or eleventh century, or from a tribe of Tartars driven eastward across Behring's Straits by the Aleoutski Islands, during the tyranny of Zengis Khan; the state of things exhibited by the Indian nations and the Indian languages of America, on the discovery of that continent by Europeans, being altogether irreconcileable with the supposition of so recent an origin. America was undoubtedly peopled many ages before Julius Cæsar landed in Britain; and the colossal structures of his forefathers, that still excite the wonder of the wandering Indian of Peru, were in all likelihood in ruins long before the great grandfather of the Tartar conqueror was born.

I have shown above that the original discoverers of America must have landed on the west coast of that continent, somewhere near Copiapo, in the State of Chili, in the very earliest period of the history of mankind. Their immediate descendants travelling northward and southward, along the western slope of the Cordilleras, formed powerful and flourishing empires in both continents, far surpassing in point of civilization the more recent empires of Montezuma and the Incas of Peru. In these empires, all the knowledge and civilization that had survived the immense voyage across the Pacific Ocean were preserved and turned to account; but it seems doubtful whether the scion from the tree of knowledge which had thus been transplanted from Eastern Asia, and which evidently maintained its Asiatic life for many centuries, ever shot forth any additional branches in the American soil, with the exception perhaps of the astronomical attainments and picture writings of the ancient Mexicans. The Mississippi—*the gathering of the waters*, as the word is said to signify in the Indian language—would serve as the grand conductor of civilization to the tribes that in successive ages advanced to the northward; and hence we find the remains of Indian *tumuli* and of Indian forts along the banks of the Ohio, and in the immediate vicinity of the lakes of Canada. But the dense forests of the Brazils, the pampas of La Plata, and the wilds of Patagonia were evidently less favourable for the preservation of the habitudes of Indian civilization; and hence we observe a gradual deterioration of the Indian race among the tribes that diverged into these regions from the parent settlements of the southern continent, till at length the wretched Brazilian cannibal, or the miserable inhabitant of Tierra del Fuego— paddling in his rude canoe in search of whale-blubber along the stormy headlands of his inhospitable isle—scarcely exhibits any evidence of his ancient descent from the bold adventurous Malay, who had steered his beautifully carved galley from island to island across the vast Pacific, carrying along with him the knowledge and the primitive civilization of the East.

The aborigines of America were found, at the era of its discovery by the Spaniards, scattered over the length and breadth of a vast continent, extending from the Atlantic to the Pacific, from Hudson's Bay to the Straits of Le Maire; and they were broken up, moreover, into an infinity of tribes speaking an infinity of tongues. To effect this wide dispersion, and to give rise to this wonderful diversity of languages, America, as I have just observed, must have been discovered and settled by its aboriginal inhabitants at the very earliest period in the history of the world. That a period, however, of from three to four thousand years is quite sufficient to explain the phenomena to which I have just alluded, I have no doubt whatever. I have already observed that that eminent American statesman and philologist, the Hon. Albert Gallatin, a native of Geneva, but a naturalized subject of the American Union from the days of Washington, is entirely of the same opinion.

Before proceeding with the discussion of the question as to whether there is anything in the phenomena of language in North America to form an insuperable objection to the theory of this work, viz., that the Indo-Americans are all originally of one race, and that they all came from Polynesia, I would observe that the great Polynesian language exhibits the strongest relations, not only with the Malayan language of the Indian Archipelago, as we have seen above, but with the Chinese and Indo-Chinese languages of Eastern Asia.

The Chinese and Polynesian languages therefore are in great measure monosyllabic, i.e., a great proportion of the primitive words or units of thought in both languages are monosyllables. In the Polynesian dialects every word ends in a vowel: this, it is true, is not the case in the

Chinese; but it would seem that in the latter, which is the language of the more civilized people, the final vowel has, in many cases, been dropped, just as the final *e* of the Saxon or Teutonic language has become mute in modern English. Thus the word *tong*, which in Chinese signifies *east*, is in the language of New Zealand *tonga*, which, I apprehend, is its more ancient form.

Mr. Marsden uniformly represents the Polynesian dialects as being radically polysyllabic. A slight inspection of any of their vocabularies will be sufficient to convince the intelligent reader, that a large proportion of the words of these dialects consists either of monosyllables, or of polysyllables, each of the component parts of which forms a distinct word. The Chinese language itself by no means abhors such compounds.

In both languages words are susceptible of no change whatever to denote diversity of gender, number, case, or what is understood in European languages by declension and conjugation. Every possible increment of thought must be expressed by a separate word—in no instance by a mere change of termination. Thus *nyan*, a man (Chinese, Canton dialect); *nu nyan*, a woman; *to hunga*, a priest (New Zealand;) *e tane to hunga*, a male priest; *e wahine to hunga*, a female priest or priestess. The plural in the New Zealand dialect is formed by prefixing *nga*; as *ika*, a fish; *nga ika*, fishes; in Chinese it is formed by adding *men* (probably *mena* originally) as *ta*, he; *ta men*, they. Nay, in both languages the same word is either a noun or a verb, according to the particles it has conjoined with it; as *ngo siang*, I think (Chinese); *ngo ti siang*, my thought.

Relationship is expressed, and compound words or ideas are formed, in both languages, by the mere juxta-position of primitive words. Thus:—

| CHINESE. | | MALAY AND POLYNESIAN. | |
|---|---|---|---|
| Tao | Head | Ka-too (Island of Savu) | Head. |
| Tao-faa | Hair of the head. | Ru-katoo | Hair of the head. |
| Sao | Hand. | Mata | Eye. |
| Sao-tchee | Finger. | Mata orang | Man's eye. |
| Sao-tchee-ong | Thumb. | Orang timor | Men of the east. |

Particles are used in both languages in a similar way; and these particles are in many instances not merely similar, but absolutely identical. The particle *e* or *y* (which in Chinese signifies *one*) is prefixed to nouns both in the Chinese and Polynesian languages; so also is the particle *ko* or *ka*; thus:—

| Chinese. | | Polynesian. | |
|---|---|---|---|
| Y ko nyan | A man. | E manu | A bird. |
| Y ko nu-nyan | A woman. | E dima | Five. |
| Y ko chu | A tree. | E ko nai | The chin. |
| Y ko mi | A grain of rice. | E ko hu | A fog. |
| Ko tyan | The heel. | Ko tiro | A girl. |
| Ko tyee | The toes. | Ko ta | A shell. |
| Ko tsau | The blood. | Ko taha | A war instrument. |

It is not allowable, however, either in the language of China or in that of the South Sea Islands, to use the same particle in conjunction with any noun. On the contrary, the particle is varied according to the signification of the noun with which it is conjoined. Thus it would be improper to say, although in apparent accordance with the examples already given, *y ko tao*, a sword; *y ko ma*, a horse; *y ko hoa*, a flower.

In accordance with the recommendation of our own great master of languages in a somewhat similar case. "He who would speak the language of the celestial empire with the requisite propriety, and acquire a Chinese style classical without pedantry, and copious without redundance, must say, *y pa tao; y pi ma; y to hoa.*" All these three particles, however, (viz., *pa*, *pe*, or *pi to*) are used in exactly the same manner in the Polynesian dialects; as, for instance, *e pa di* (New Zealand dialect), a precipice; *e pa kéha*,* a white man or European: *e po* or *pe tiki*, a younger brother; *e pe pe*, a butterfly; *e to ki*, an axe; *e to hunga*, a priest. Such coincidences cannot possibly be accidental; they are far less equivocal than coincidences in the meaning of particular words in the two languages. In both languages, also, the same particles are used in the formation of what may be termed the moods

---

* The New Zealanders allege that the flea, which, it seems, is not an indigenous inhabitant of their island, but a sort of free emigrant intruder, was introduced by the English, and they consequently designate it *e pa keha nohi nohi, the little European.*

and tenses of the verb; such as *pa, pe, te.* *Hoei,* which in Chinese forms the future tense, appears in the form of *gooa* in the dialect of the Friendly Islands, of *hoi* in that of the Society Islands, and of *koa* in that of New Zealand. The very aspect of the Chinese and Polynesian verbs is sufficient of itself to afford a presumption of affinity in their languages: thus:—

| CHINESE. | | POLYNESIAN (NEW ZEALAND). | |
| --- | --- | --- | --- |
| Pa pou te ngo ngai | O that I might love. | Koa kai ke pe oki au | I might have eaten. |
| Ngo pi ta ngai | I am loved by him. | E kai ana koe | Thou eatest. |

It were quite impossible for us Westerns to ascertain the particular increment of thought these particles individually express or represent; but this is not peculiar to the case of the eastern languages. It would be somewhat difficult for us to ascertain what Homer meant by the Greek particle ρα, which he uses so frequently when we think he might have done as well without it. I have heard of a learned member of one of the English universities, who was rather puzzled with that particle, translating Homer's phrase Τρωες ρα,—The Trojans, God bless them!

Similar, and these remarkably peculiar, sounds abound in both languages. Consonantal sounds are much less numerous in the Chinese and Polynesian languages than in those of Europe and Western Asia; and the number of vowel sounds is consequently much greater. Words which in Roman characters would be represented by the very same combinations of letters, are found to have the most opposite significations; the accentuation, and the depth, strength, or weakness of the intonation of the vowel sound, rendering what appears to a European the same word, susceptible of a variety of meanings, or, rather, originating a whole series of different words. This peculiarity, the reader will doubtless perceive, is much more likely to originate endless varieties of dialect than the consonantal languages of Europe, in which the landmarks or consonants are not so easily got over or worn down. Hence it has actually happened that, while the written language of China is universally intelligible, not only in China Proper and in the provinces of Chinese Tartary, but also in Japan and in Cochin-China—every province, every city, nay, almost every village of the Celestial Empire, has its own peculiar dialect, which, according to the Jesuits of the Propaganda mission, is often scarcely intelligible beyond its own narrow limits. On the other hand, while the tendency in the Chinese language seems to have been to get rid of final vowels, the tendency in some of the Polynesian dialects has been to get rid of consonants, and to reduce the language to a series of endless combinations of vowel sounds. The nasal sound, *ng*, is remarkably prevalent, both in the beginning and at the end of words, in the languages of China and Polynesia. Thus:—

| CHINESE. | | POLYNESIAN (NEW ZEALAND). | |
|---|---|---|---|
| Ngaa* | Teeth. | Nganga | Skull. |
| Ngaan | Eyes. | Ngako | Fat. |
| Ngo | I. | Ngutu (Utu, Tahit.) | Lip. |
| Tchuong | Long. | Rangi | Heaven |
| Tung | Brass. | Tangi | Cry. |

* In the Tahitian dialect, in which the nasal sound becomes a guttural intonation, the word for *teeth* is *niho*. I conceive it is the same as the Chinese word.

In the Polynesian dialects, *t* and *k* are convertible, and so also are *l*, *r*, and *d*. *Ariki, a conjuror,* in the New Zealand dialect, becomes *Arii,* with a guttural intonation, in the dialect of Otaheite; while *Tangata,* a man, becomes *Taata,* with a similar intonation, marking the place of the lost consonantal sound. This intonation is so peculiar as to impress the person who hears it for the first time with the idea that the vowel sound has stuck in the speaker's throat.

6. Various words are of the same signification in both languages. Thus:—

| CHINESE. | | POLYNESIAN. | |
|---|---|---|---|
| T'hai | The sea. | Tai | The sea. |
| I'u* | Fish. | I'yu (Tahitian)* | Fish. |
| Yu | Rain. | Ua | Rain. |
| Tong | East. | Tonga | East. |
| Ngau | Bite. | Ngau | Bite (gnaw). |
| Nga-dow | Brow. | Nga-du | Wave, q.d. Brow of the sea. |
| How | Mouth. | Vaha (Tahitian) | Mouth. |
| Ko tsau | Blood. | To Tu (Tahitian) | Blood. |

* The guttural intonation is the same in both cases. In the Malayan and New Zealand dialects the consonant is preserved, and the word is pronounced *ika*.

These coincidences occur in a comparatively small number of words, from each of the two languages under review. I am confident, however, that if the investigation were pursued, hundreds of words might be found in the Chinese language nearly, if not entirely, coincident in signification with words of exactly similar sound in one or other of the numerous dialects of the Polynesian tongue. At all events, I conceive there is reason to conclude, that both the nations and the languages of China and Polynesia have sprung from the same ancient and prolific source; and that the line of demarcation which Professor Blumenbach has attempted to draw between the Mongolian and the Malayan races of mankind, is purely imaginary.

In a very learned, but unfortunately posthumous work of the late Baron William Humboldt, a brother of the illustrious traveller, entitled "Ueber die Kawi Sprache im inseln Java," "on the Kauri language in the island of Java," copies of which are to be found in our Parliamentary and University libraries, that eminent philologist informs us how polysyllabic are formed from monosyllabic languages by the mere process of aggregation—a process which can be much more easily carried out in a vocalic than in a consonantal tongue; as seems to have been the case in great measure with the Polynesian language.

It may not be out of place to remark in passing that we have a large monosyllabic element in our own English language, and that the process of of converting that monosyllabic into a polysillabic element is effected in the very way Baron William Humboldt informs us characterises the process in the East, viz., by mere aggregation, without any change in either of the words combined. Thus, from the English monosyllable *eye*, we have the dissyllables *eye-lid*, *eye-lash*, *eye-brow*, *eye-sore*, by the simple process of aggregation. From nose, we have *nosegay;* from cheek, *cheekbone;* from mouth, *mouthpiece;* from head, *head-dress* and *headache;* from hair, *hair-brush*, *hair-comb*, *hair-oil*, &c., &c., &c. In short, we do a large business in English with our monosyllables; and we often excite the envy of our French cousins of literary taste who have no such facilities in that way. The German language has doubtless great powers in the way of combination, and presents us ever and anon with as formidable compounds as the sesquipedalian words of the North American Indians. To instance only two of these—there is *religions-verbesserung*, the bettering of religion or reformation; and *schneidersgesellschaft*, Journeymen Tailors' Society. But our English monosyllabic combinations are far simpler and far more suitable.

To return to our proper subject from this digression—which, however, we shall find of some practical use in the sequel—the American literati had concluded, I believe universally, that their two continents had been originally discovered and occupied, at different times and at different points, by totally different people, and that there was not even the shadow of a community of language between them. But, to use a sea phrase, they were "taken all aback" at once when it was ascertained, about forty or fifty years since, that there was actually an Indo-American tribe or nation inhabiting the mountains of Mexico—the veritable Indo-American capital of North America—and speaking a language unquestionably monosyllabic, and presenting the same relations to the Chinese and Indo-Chinese languages of Eastern Asia as I have shown the Polynesian dialects do generally. The people I allude to are the Ottomies, and their language is called the Ottomie language. An account both of the people and their language is contained in a paper in Latin, published at Philadelphia, in the Journal of the American Philosophical Society for 1835, of which a copy was sent me so early as the year 1836, by my late friend, John Pickering, Esq., of Boston, one of the most distinguished philologists of North America. It is entitled, *De Lingua Othomitorum Dissertatio; Auctore Emmanuele Naxera, Mexicano, Academiæ Litterariæ Zacatecarum Socio*—A Dissertation on the Language of the Ottomies; by Emanuel Naxera, a Mexican, Fellow of the Literary Academy of Zacatecas. The Ottomies are not a numerous people, but they have always been in a state of antagonism or hostility, both towards the native

Government before the Conquest, and ever since to the Spaniards, by whom they allege they have been much persecuted.

The learned Spaniard who published this Dissertation in Philadelphia, I may observe in passing, was a refugee or political exile at the time from his unhappy country, to which, however, he appears to have been devotedly attached. He gives us first, as a specimen of the language, the Lord's Prayer, as follows, in the Ottomie dialect:—

1. Ma thâ he ni bùy mahētsi
2. Da ne ansū ni hūhū
3. Da ēhē ga he ni bùy
4. Da kha ni hnee
5. Ngù wa na hày
6. Te ngù mahētsi
7. Ma hmē he ta nâ pa
8. Râ he na ra pa ya
9. Ha puni he
10. Ma dupatè he
11. Tēngù di puni he
12. U ma ndupatè he
13. Ha yo wi hē he

1. Noster pater habitas cœlum
2. Vocabunt sanctum tuum nomen,
3. Veniet ergà nos tua habitatio,
4. Facient tua voluntas
5. Et ità hic terra
6. Sicut cœlum
7. Noster panis quæque dies (cujusque diei)
8. Da nos unus dies nova (hodiè)
9. Et parce nos.
10. Nostra debita
11. Sicut nos parcimus
12. Nunc debitores nostri
13. Et cave ne permittere nos

| | |
|---|---|
| 14. Ga he kha na tzò cadi | 14. Labemur in turpis actio |
| 15. Ma na pehe he hin nhò | 15. Sed salva nos non bonum (à non bono) |
| 16. Dak ha. | 16. Facient (hoc est *Amen*.) |

Signor Naxera next points out, from repeated references to the Chinese grammar of the great French Oriental scholar, M. Remusat (as I have done in the case of the Polynesian language generally) a whole series of points in which the Ottomie dialect coincides with the Chinese; and last, but not least, he shows us that, in common with the Indo-Chinese nations, the Polynesian and the Mexican portion of the Indo-American race, the Ottomies have a language of ceremony or reverence distinct from the language of common life. For example, instead of saying in the common language, as one would do to an equal, "You are asleep," if addressing a superior, either in Church or State, the phraseology must be—

| Rzu | ki | i a |
|---|---|---|
| Altitudo | venerabilis | dormit |

The venerable altitude (or Highness) sleeps.

In one word, I consider this case of the Ottomies the strongest imaginable to prove the identity of the Polynesian and Indo-American nations. That such a people, with such a language as that of the Ottomies, could ever have come from the northern portion of North America is altogether inconceivable. The only way of accounting both for their place and their tongue is that they had passed over to America from one of the islands of the Southern Pacific. It follows, therefore, that instead of there being any insuperable objections to my theory in the phenomena of language in North America, there is the very strongest evidence in its favour.

## CHAPTER X.

**THE INDO-AMERICANS ARE NOT ABORIGINES, IN THE SENSE OF BEING A DISTINCT CREATION FROM THE REST OF MANKIND, BUT ARE RELATED, IN THE WAY OF NATURAL DESCENT, TO ANOTHER LARGE DIVISION OF THE FAMILY OF MAN.**

During the past fifty years it has been a growing opinion among literary and scientific men, and especially among travellers in America, if at all predisposed to scepticism, that the Indo-Americans are indigenous, or a separate creation, altogether distinct from the rest of mankind. The following are a few specimens of this character: "I am compelled," says Mr. Catlin, the author of two interesting volumes of travels among the Indians of North America, "I am compelled to believe that the continent of America, and each of the other continents, have had their aboriginal stocks, peculiar in colour and in character, and that each of these native stocks has undergone repeated mutations by erratic colonies from abroad."* "We can never know the origin of the Americans," says M. Morlet, a French writer; "the theory that they are aborigines is contradicted by no fact, and is plausible enough."† "The supposition," says another American traveller, "that the Red Man is a primitive type of a human family originally planted in the Western Continent, presents the most natural solution of this problem. The researches of physiologists, antiquaries, philologists, tend this way. The hypothesis of an immigration, when followed out, is embarrassed with great difficulties, and leads to interminable and unsatisfying speculations."‡ "The unsuccessful search after traces of an ante-Columbian intercourse with the New World suffices to confirm the belief that, for unnumbered centuries throughout that ancient era, the western hemisphere was the exclusive heritage of nations native to its

---

*Catlin, "North American Indians," vol. II., page 232.
† "Morlet's, Voyages," tom. 1, page 177.
‡ "Norman's Rambles in Yucatan," page 251.

soil."* Dr. Morton concludes "that the American race differs essentially from all others, not excepting the Mongolian; nor do the feeble analogies of language, and the more obvious ones in civil and religious institutions, and the arts, denote anything beyond casual and colonial communication with the Asiatic nations; and even these analogies may perhaps be accounted for, as Humboldt has suggested, in the mere coincidence arising from similar wants and impulses in nations inhabiting similar latitudes."†

"Altemirano, the best Aztec scholar living, claims that the proof is conclusive that the Aztecs did not come here from Asia, as has been almost universally believed, but were a race originated in America, and as old as the Chinese themselves, and that China may even have been peopled from America."‡ Swan, in his work entitled "The North-West Coast," believes "that whatever was the origin of different tribes or

---

\* " Wilson's Prehistoric Man," page 421.
† " Crania Americana," page 260.
‡ Evans, " Our Sister Republics," page 333.

families, the whole race of American Indians are native and indigenous to the soil.*

Mr. Bancroft, to whom I am indebted for certain of these references, and who virtually adopts the theory of the Americans being indigenous, observes as follows: " The preceding resumé shews pretty conclusively that the American people, and the American civilization, if not indigenous to the New World, were introduced from the Old at a period long preceding any to which we are carried by the traditional or monumental annals of either continent. We have found no evidence of any populating or civilizing migration across the ocean, from east to west, north or south, within historic times. Nothing approaching identity has been discovered between any two nations separated by the Atlantic or Pacific. No positive record appears even of communication between America and the Old World—intentional by commercial, exploring, or warlike expeditions, or by shipwreck—previous to the voyages of the Northmen of the tenth

---
* Page 206.

century; *yet that such communication did take place in many instances, and at different periods, is extremely probable.*" Begging Mr. Bancroft's pardon, I cannot think such communication probable at all, and no person who has traversed both of the largest oceans in the world—the Pacific and Atlantic---very much, like myself, could ever think so. When the forefathers of the Indo-American race were separated from the rest of mankind, they were so, for themselves and their descendants, for ever; the idea of any communication having ever existed between them and the old world, across either of these vast oceans, is, in my humble opinion, utterly improbable, and entirely unwarranted.

Such, then, are man's thoughts in regard to the origin of the Indo-American nations, and their dispersion over the great continent which it is admitted they have inhabited for so many past generations. They are indigenous, and were either created, or, to use the current phraseology of the new philosophy, *developed* from some inferior specimen of the animal creation. But such are evidently not God's thoughts in this matter—He made the earth to be inhabited, and, in order to carry out that purpose, He brought inhabitants to occupy the American part of it across the broadest part of the Pacific Ocean, in a way that would never have been thought of by any of the sons of men: for His thoughts are not our thoughts, nor His ways our ways. There is, happily, therefore, no necessity for searching for another Adam, to give inhabitants to America. This great desideratum has been provided by Infinite Wisdom, in the way I have indicated; for the Polynesians and the Indo-Americans are the same people, and the same God made them both.

Mr. Bancroft mentions a singular circumstance, strongly confirmatory of my theory in this matter: " Three traditions," he observes, " are especially prevalent, in some form, in nearly every section of America—that of a Deluge—that of an Aboriginal migration, and that of giants having dwelt upon the earth at some time in the remote past;"* for, if the emigration of

---

* " The Native Races of the Pacific States of North America." By Hubert Howe Bancroft, London, 1876.—Vol. V., page 138.

the forefathers of the Polynesian race from the Plains of Shinar, to the eastward, took place, as we have supposed it did, very shortly after the Deluge, the story of that great catastrophe, as well as of their own subsequent migration, would be indelibly impressed upon their minds, and carried with them as their most cherished tradition, wherever they went. We have already seen, from their carrying with them, through all their wanderings, the idea of a great Spirit, invisible to men, that they had taken their departure from the rest of mankind before the knowledge and worship of one living and true God had disappeared and perished from amongst men. And that the form and character of the earliest post-diluvian religious edifices should have been so strongly photographed upon the national mind as, after a whole series of successive voyages across the Pacific, to be reproduced in the Marais of Tahiti, and the Teocallis of Mexico, is one of the most remarkable facts in the history of mankind. But as to the third of the universally prevalent traditions of the Indo-

American people, viz., that a race of giants existed on the earth in the earlier post-diluvian ages, I would not offer any decided opinion on the subject, as there is something, doubtless, to be said on both sides.

There are a few points, however, in reference to the facts and history of Polynesian and Indo-American civilization to which I have not yet adverted, from their bearing but lightly on the main question of this work, but on which I would offer a few observations before bringing the subject to a close. I would observe, therefore, that remains of ancient and regular fortifications have from time to time been discovered in both continents of America; and the circumstance has repeatedly awakened much curiosity respecting the origin, the history, and the fate of the nation that has left behind it these memorials of its ancient civilization. But regular fortifications of a similar kind are still met with in all parts of the South Sea Islands. In some islands they are constructed of walls of loose stones piled on each other on the tops of hills, as in New

Zealand; in others, they are formed of strong palisades, like the Burman stockades, as in the level island of Tonga: and in others again they consist of some artificial addition to a place of great natural strength, as in the district of Atehuru, in Tahiti. In short, the South Sea Islanders have evidently been in a sufficiently advanced state of civilization, in ages past, to enable them to construct fortifications, and to adapt these fortifications, in regard to the materials employed in their construction, to the nature of the country in which they were required. Those of the Indo-Americans appear to have been generally formed of mounds of earth—a mode of formation well adapted for such localities as the alluvial banks of the Ohio, the dead levels near the lakes of Canada, or the elevated plains of central America, but not at all adapted for the South Sea Islands.*

---

* My talented townsman, the late John Galt, Esq., of Greenock, has informed me that he has seen the remains of an Indian fort on the summit of a precipitous ridge near Lake Simcoe, in Upper Canada. It consisted of a mound of earth, enclosing a considerable extent of ground; but on the banks of the Miamis River, much farther to the southward, the Indian forts have been constructed of stone. Have any such forts, I would ask, been discovered in Kamtschatka?

Nay, the march of ancient civilization among the Indo-Americans may even be traced, in some measure, by these most interesting remains. In South America I have not heard of their being found to the eastward of the Andes. The gloomy forests of Guiana and the Brazils were evidently unfavourable for the preservation of Indo-American civilization; and the portion of the race that wandered into these vast solitudes was necessarily broken up, at an early period, into an infinity of insignificant tribes that could hold little or no communication with each other, and that, consequently, very soon sunk irrecoverably beneath the level of the rest of their nation. But the regions of central America, the elevated plains of Bogota and Cundinamarca, the open valleys of Peru, and the lofty and secluded, but highly fertile, tracts of Chili, were much more favourable for the formation and maintenance of powerful states and empires; and it is, accordingly, in these portions of the continent of South America that the ruins of ancient cities and of extensive fortifications are found.* In

---

\* M. Kenous, a Danish traveller, has recently discovered ruins of the kind above-mentioned in the Chilian Andes.

the North American continent, the course of the Mississippi and its tributary streams would, doubtless, guide the Indian in his progress to the northward ; and it is, accordingly, on the banks of the Ohio, in the western prairies, and along the lakes of Canada, that we find the monuments of his ancient power.

Again, the picture-writing of the ancient Mexicans, of which the late Lord Kingsborough has given us so splendid a collection of specimens in his magnificent but purposeless work, "The Monuments of Mexico," had unquestionably a decidedly Polynesian, Malayan, or Chinese aspect. Although the Malayan nations inhabiting the islands of the Indian Archipelago were possessed of a written language, with an alphabetic character, long anterior to the rise and prevalence of the Portuguese empire in the east, that incontestible evidence of superior civilization must doubtless be regarded as one of those improvements that were derived, according to Sir Stamford Raffles, at an early period in the history of the nation, through the medium of the Sanscrit language, from the more civilized Indian nations to the westward of the Ganges. There is reason to believe, however, that long anterior to the introduction of alphabetic writing, the Malays, in common with the other branches of their widely-extended nation, were not unacquainted with a more imperfect method of communicating their ideas, and of transmitting a record of passing events to posterity. The present written language of China is merely an improved edition of the primitive hieroglyphical writing of ancient Egypt—a sort of halfway station in the progress of the human mind towards an alphabet; and there is reason to believe that, at the period when the Polynesian nation began to people the multitude of the isles, that more ancient and imperfect species of communication was in general use among the Chinese, the Indo-Chinese, and the Malayan divisions of the Mongolian race.

" In the course of our tour around Hawaii," says the Rev. Mr. Ellis, in an Appendix to his valuable work entitled Polynesian Researches, " we met with a few specimens of what may perhaps be termed the first efforts of an uncivilized people towards the construction of a language of symbols. Along the southern coast, both on the east and west sides, we frequently saw a number of straight lines, semi-circles, or concentric rings, with some rude imitations of the human figure, cut or carved in the compact rocks of lava. They did not appear to have been cut with an iron instrument, but with a stone hatchet, or a stone less frangible than the rock on which they were pourtrayed. On inquiry, we found that they had been made by former travellers, from a motive similar to that which induces a person to carve his initials on a stone or tree, or a traveller to record his name in an album—to inform his successors that he has been there. When there were a number of concentric circles with a dot or mark in the centre, the dot signified a man, and the number of rings denoted the number in the party who had circumambulated the island. When there was a ring, and a number of marks, it denoted the same; the number of marks showing of how many the party consisted; and the ring, that they had travelled completely round the island; but when there was only a semi-circle, it denoted that they had returned after reaching the place where it was made. In some of the islands we have seen the outline of a fish pourtrayed in the same manner, to denote that one of that species or size had been taken near the spot; sometimes the dimensions of an exceedingly large fruit, &c., are marked in the same way."*

The Indian nations of North America had carried this as well as the other arts, and the general civilization of its central regions, as high as the lakes of Canada. When that province was colonized by the French, the most powerful Indian nation in North America were the Iroquois—a nation whom it afterwards required many a fierce battle to exterminate. That warlike nation was sufficiently civilized at the period I refer to to practice the Mexican art of picture-writing; for an Indian village, situated somewhere near the site of the present city of Montreal, having about that period been surprised and destroyed by the

---

* "Polynesian Researches," vol. iv., p. 459.

French, a painting or picture-writing, which afterwards fell into the hands of the French, containing a hieroglyphical representation of the event, was executed by some Indian artist, to transmit an account of it either to the distant tribes of the nation or to posterity. The village was indicated by a series of wigwams, and the state in which its inhabitants were surprised, by an Indian asleep. The rising sun indicated that the attack had taken place at the break of day; and the moon in her first quarter, mounted on the back of a stag, afforded the additional information that it had taken place in the early part of the month in the Indian year of which the stag was the emblem.*

In a letter to the secretary of the Antiquarian Society, published in the sixth volume of the

---

* I recollect listening with a feeling of intense interest to an account of this picture-writing which was given in the course of a Lecture on Natural and Artificial Signs, delivered in the Logic or First Philosophy Class, by the late eminent Professor Jardine, of the University of Glasgow, in the year 1813. In recurring to such scenes, one cannot help sympathising with the grateful feelings which the poet Vida expresses to his deceased parents, for having sent him from his native city when very young to a college at Rome :—

Me puerum docilem doctam misistis ad urbem.

Archæology, W. Bray, Esq., gives an account of an Indian picture writing which had been intended to commemorate the exploits of Wingenund, an Indian warrior of the Delaware nation, about the middle of last century. It consisted of a series of marks or characters inscribed within a square figure on a sugar maple-tree on the Muskingham River in the State of Delaware. The first line consisted of the figure of a turtle—the emblem of the tribe to which the warrior belonged—an arbitrary mark designating the particular chief who had executed the writing, and a representation of the sun. Ten horizontal lines on the right side of the figure denoted the number of expeditions in which the warrior had been engaged, and opposite to each of these lines on the left there was a series of marks resembling the letter X, with a bar across the top of it, representing the number of scalps or of prisoners he had taken, the sex of the victim being designated by a slight variation of the character, and the central part of the figure being occupied with a rude drawing of three different British forts which he had attacked on these occasions. At the bottom of the figure there were twenty-three vertical lines inclining a little to the left (the figure of the sun in the first line of the writing being at the right side of the painting) to denote that at the same time the record was left the writer was marching on another expedition to the northward.

A similar mode of communication is in use among the Indians of the present day still farther to the northward. " The next day," says the Rev. John West, A.M., late chaplain to the Honorable the Hudson's Bay Company, in his Narrative of a Journey undertaken within the territory of the Red River Colony in the year 1820, " we forded Broad River, on the banks of which we saw several dens, which the bears had scratched for shelter; and seeing the smoke of an Indian tent at some distance before us, in the direction we were going, we quickened our step, and reached it before we stopped to breakfast. We found the whole family clothed in deer-skins, and upon a hunting excursion from Church-hill. The Indian, or rather a half-breed, was very communicative, and told me that, although he was leading an Indian life, his father was formerly a master at one of the Company's posts, and proposed accompanying our party to the factory. He had two sons, he said, who were gone in the pursuit of a deer ; and, on quitting the encampment to travel with us, he would leave some signs for them to follow us on their return. They were drawn upon a broad piece of wood which he prepared with an axe. They were—1st, a tent struck, to intimate that the party had gone forward in a particular direction ; 2nd, five rude figures, indicating the number of the party, and exhibiting by their dress and accoutrements the rank or condition of each individual, viz.: a European chief, a European servant, an Indian attendant, and two Indians from the encampment ; 3rd, a curvilinear figure, with the two extremities of the curve pointing towards the hindermost of the figures, to intimate to the Indian's two sons that they were to follow the party."*

---

* The substance of a Journal during a residence at the Red River colony ; by John West, M.A. London, 1824.

The picture-writing of the Mexicans constituted the annals of their empire; and we are assured on reliable authority that these annals formed a continuous history of the country to as high a period as the sixth century of the Christian era. It is unquestionable, however, that the pyramids and other ancient monuments, both of Peru and Mexico, are the remains of a primitive and Asiatic civilization which had run its course and become extinct long before either the Aztecks or the Toltics were heard of in the world. That there had been a renaissance, however, of that ancient and higher civilization under these Mexican people, just as there was in our own world after the era of the Crusades and the fall of Constantinople, is equally evident.

I would also observe, without intending the slightest reflection on our Legislative Assembly for its somewhat different practice, that the great councils of the Indo-American nations, in which affairs of public interest were publicly discussed, were conducted in the same manner as those of the Polynesian nation. Youth was not suffered to mingle in the high debate. Regular harangues were delivered, most of which were highly animated, and some highly eloquent. And when any Speaker had possession of the Assembly, he was listened to with profound attention. All such attempts to put down an obnoxious orator as *coughing*, cries of *hear, oh! question*, &c., would have absolutely shocked the right feelings of the Polynesian and the Indo-American, cannibals though they were.

From the preceding notices it will doubtless appear that the Indians of North America are derived from the same prolific source as the aborigines of the southern continent; and the entire dissimilarity of the whole framework of their singularly formed society to anything of European origin, sufficiently demonstrates the absurdity of those hypotheses that would trace the aborigines of either continent to ancient colonies from Norway or from Wales—with the exception, perhaps, of the Greenlanders of the far North, to whom I have alluded above. Columbus was undoubtedly the first European that ever crossed the Atlantic or trod American ground; and that great man was not diaappointed, as we commonly suppose him to have been, in the attainment of his original object—the discovery of a shorter route to the East Indies. It was the Indians of Cathay that he actually found in the Island of Hispaniola. He had there reached the easternmost of the settlements of that great nation, whose innumerable tribes had for thousands of years been the sole occupants of nearly half the surface of the globe.

From the evidence I have adduced, in the previous chapters of this work, to prove the unity and identity of the Indo-American nations, and their derivation, by natural descent, from the Polynesians of the vast Pacific Ocean, as well as from the utter want of evidence to prove that there had ever been any immigration from Asia to America, either before or since the western discovery of that continent by Captain Behring, it will scarcely be necessary to enter upon a formal confutation of any of the numerous theories that have been put forth by the learned during the last three centuries, on the supposition of such an emigration having actually taken place. The Indo-Americans are neither aborigines nor a distinct creation, but simply the descendants of the handful of famished Polynesians who, when driven off their own island by a violent gale of westerly wind, had landed on the South American coast, from Easter Island, somewhere near Copiapo, in the State of Chili, a few hundred years after the deluge, carrying with them, and re-producing in America, the fashions of the day, especially in architecture, in that early period of the history of mankind.

It was no wonder, however, that neither Humboldt nor Dr. Robertson was of a different opinion, and accordingly supposed that they had traced the Indo-Americans to North-Eastern Asia; for, until a comparatively recent period, when the Polynesians and their monuments in the great Pacific Ocean came to be known to Europeans through the discoveries of our great English and French navigators, it would doubtless have appeared to men of science and learning as utterly incredible that America had been originally discovered and settled from South America as it would have been that its first discoverers had come from the moon. But " God's thoughts in these matters are not as our thoughts, neither are His ways our ways."

In regard to the Japanese consul of San Francisco, and his recent advocacy of the theory of De Zuniga, which he supports by alleging that vessels from Japan had been wrecked on the west coast of North America, and may therefore have given its aboriginal population to that continent, there is not the slightest evidence in favour of such a supposition; and when the problem can be solved satisfactorily and without conjecture in another way, as this work will doubtless prove it can, there is no necessity for attempting a different solution. The following is an instance of a Japanese junk having been found in the last state of exhaustion in the route from China and Japan to San Francisco, which I extract from the news of the day in the *Sydney Morning Herald* of the period, although it affords but little encouragement for the idea of any communication having ever been maintained between Japan and North America.

POLYNESIA.—On the 12th June, 1871, the Pacific Mail Steamship, China, on her voyage from China to San Francisco, fell in with a Japanese junk, in lat. 34 deg. 54 min. N., and long. 143 deg. 42 min. E., which had been driven off the coast [of Japan], dismasted and rudderless, eleven men having died on board of starvation ; the twelfth, as one of four rescued in the last stage of exhaustion, dying the day after arriving in San Francisco.

This case sufficiently shows that there are sudden and violent gales from the westward in the Northern as well as in the Southern Pacific ; but it is proper to state that the unfortunate junk was still three thousand miles from the American coast when fallen in with by the mail steamer.

In regard to the expedition of the Welch Prince Madoc, who, we are told, had an expedition of ten ships, which crossed the Atlantic to America, in the tenth or eleventh century, I cannot believe that such an expedition ever took place. Mr. Catlin, however, the American traveller, not only supposes that it did, but is strongly inclined to believe, also, that Madoc and his ten ships entered the Mississippi and passed up that river till its junction with the Missouri. He then ascended both the Missouri and one of its tributaries, the Yellowstone River, where he founded, through his followers, a Welch colony on the latter River, which we are to believe is represented by the Mandans, an Indo-American tribe settled on the Upper Missouri, and subsisting to the present day. "I have been disposed," says Mr. Catlin, " to enquire whether here may not be found yet existing the remains of the Welch colony, the followers of Madoc, who, history tells us, started with ten ships to colonize a country which he had discovered in the Western Ocean—whose expedition I think has been pretty clearly traced to the mouth of the Mississippi, or the coast of Florida, and whose fate, further than this, seems sealed in unsearchable mystery."*

---

* "Letters and Notes on the Manners, Customs, and Condition of the North American Indians." By George Catlin. London : 1841. Page 206.

But Mr. Catlin ignores two very important circumstances in the case which he ought to have remembered; for the Mandans were red men, as he paints them very accurately himself, and therefore could not have been the descendants of Welchmen ; besides, who ever heard of the Welch disposing of their dead, as both the New Zealanders and Indo-Americans do, by wrapping them up in mats or skins, and placing them upon trestles, to be decomposed, and returned to their dust in the open air ? Mr. Catlin's description of this process, which I subjoin, is very interesting, but quite a refutation of his own theory on the subject.

" These people never bury the dead, but place the bodies on slight scaffolds, just above the reach of human hands, and out of the way of wolves and dogs,* and they are then left to moulder and decay. This cemetery, or place of deposit for the dead, is just back of the village, on a level prairie ; and, with all its appearances, history,

---

*It is a remarkable circumstance that the trestles for the dead in New Zealand are only about two or three feet high, because there are no wild beasts in that island.

forms, ceremonies, &c., is one of the strangest and most interesting objects to be described in the vicinity of this peculiar race.

"Whenever a person dies in the Mandan village, and the customary honours and condolence are paid to his remains, and the body dressed in the best attire, painted, oiled, feasted, and supplied with bow and quiver, shield, pipe and tobacco, knife, flint and steel, and provisions enough to last him a few days on the journey which he is to perform; a fresh buffalo's skin, just taken from the animal's back, is wrapped around the body, and tightly bound and wound, with thongs of raw hide, from head to foot; then other robes are soaked in water, till they are quite soft and elastic, which are also bandaged around the body, in like manner, and tied fast with thongs, which are wound with great care and exactness, so as to exclude the action of the air from all parts of the body. Some hundreds of these bodies may be seen reposing in this curious place, which the Indians call "the village of the dead." The Mexicans call it Micoatl.

"There is then a separate scaffold erected for it, constructed of four upright posts, a little higher than human hands can reach, and on the tops of these are small poles passing around, from one post to the others, across which a number of willow rods just strong enough to support the body, which is laid upon them on its back, with its feet carefully presented towards the rising sun. There are a great number of these bodies resting exactly in a similar way, excepting in some instances, where a chief or medicine man may be seen with a few yards of scarlet or blue cloth spread on his remains, as a mark of public respect and esteem.*

I cannot conclude this chapter without referring to the alleged ante-Columbian discovery of America by the Scandinavians, in the tenth century of our era, on which the learned Professor Rafn, of the University of Copenhagen, who patriotically advocates the claim in honour of his countrymen, has written strongly in support of it, on the authority of the Ice-

---

* Catlin—ubi supra, page 81.

landic and other northern Sagas; informing us that the place which the Norwegian discoverers had reached in their voyage along the east coast of America, somewhere between the Polar circle and the State of Florida, was called by them *Vinland*. But whether that alleged Norwegian discovery is to be received or not, the subject has just as little bearing on the previous question of this volume—the original discovery and progressive settlement of the continent of America—as another geographical and lunary question that has often been mooted, as to whether the moon is inhabited; for, as the Indo-Americans are all " red," or rather " brown" men, while no original tribe of any other colour has ever been discovered, with the exception, perhaps, of the Esquimaux, the obvious reason for so remarkable a fact is that no such tribe has ever existed ; besides, the comparatively short period that has elapsed since the alleged Scandinavian discovery, would be altogether insufficient to account for the existence of so many different languages as are now spoken in both continents of America—a phenomenon which, in my humble opinion, would require for its existence a period of not less than three or four thousand years.

The following are the sentiments of two very eminent Americans, not only on the alleged Scandinavian discovery, but also on all the others of a similar character, whether from Europe, across the Atlantic, or from North-Eastern Asia, by Behring's Straits.

"The story of the colonization of America by Northmen," observes the distinguished historian of the colonization of America, " rests on narratives mythological in form and obscure in meaning — ancient, but not contemporary. The chief document is an interpolation in the history of Sturleson, whose zealous curiosity could hardly have neglected the discovery of a continent. The geographical details are too vague to sustain a conjecture ; the accounts of the mild winter and fertile soil are, on any modern hypothesis, fictitious or exaggerated ; the description of the natives applies only to the

Esquimaux, inhabitants of hyperborean regions; the remark that should define the length of the shortest winter's day, has received interpretations adapted to every latitude from New York to Cape Farewell; and Vinland has been sought in all directions, from Greenland and the St. Lawrence, to Africa."*

The other eminent American writer, to whom I have referred, is the celebrated Washington Irving, who observes that, " as far as he had had experience in tracing these stories of early discoveries of portions of the New World, he has generally found them very confident deductions drawn from vague and questionable facts. Learned men are too prone to give substance to mere shadows, when they assist some preconceived theory. Most of these accounts, when divested of the erudite comments of their editors, have proved little better than the traditionary fables noticed in another part of this work, respecting

---

* History of the Colonization of the United States. By George Bancroft. Vol. I., pages 5 and 6.

the imaginary islands of St. Bosondon, and of the Seven Cities.*

---

* History of the Life of Columbus. By George Washington. Vol. III., page 434.

## CHAPTER XI.

### Résumé.—Plagiarism Extraordinary.—Conclusion.

Shortly after my arrival in New South Wales for the first time, in the year 1823, I became acquainted, and had much friendly intercourse, with various missionaries from the South Sea Islands, who were then, as they have always been, in the way of touching at Sydney on their voyages either out or home, as well as of occasionally visiting our city, when resident at the islands, either for health or relaxation. I was thus led to take a deep interest in the very singular inhabitants of these islands, and to institute enquiries and collect information of all kinds respecting their manners and customs, their origin and migrations. In prosecuting these enquiries, I soon satisfied myself that the South Sea Islanders or Polynesians had originally reached the Pacific from Eastern Asia and the Indian Archipelago, but *how* or *when* no man could tell.

## THE POLYNESIAN NATION. 299

In the year 1830 I happened to make a second voyage from Port Jackson to London, in connection with certain educational objects, by way of New Zealand and Cape Horn. On that voyage, after encountering a strong south-east gale right ahead of seven or eight days' continuance, off the North-East Cape of New Zealand, we were almost instantaneously caught with a violent gale from the westward, which carried us right across the Pacific to the meridian of Easter Island—the farthest east of Captain Cook's discoveries in the Pacific,* and about two thousand miles from the American Land. We then changed our course to the south-east, the westerly gale still continuing, and soon doubled Cape Horn. I mention these

---

\* Captain Cook was not the original discoverer of Pasquas or Easter Island. That, honour, is due, if I recollect aright, to the Dutch Admiral Roggewein, who discovered it some time in the seventeenth century. It was afterwards visited by an English captain Davis, from whom it was called Davis' Land; but the Spaniards, from whom we have borrowed the name, call it Pasquas or Easter Island. Captain Cook visited it in the year 1770, and astonished the world with his description of the collossal remains of a long-extinct civilization which it contains.
—Page 90.

particulars of this voyage from its having afforded me much important information, directly available, as the reader will find in the sequel, as to the course and strength of the winds in the Southern Pacific Ocean.

I had occasion to make a third voyage to England, in connection with the same objects, in the year 1833. On that voyage I had occupied myself, when crossing the Southern Pacific, in arranging and studying the papers I had collected, and the notes and extracts I had made in the colony during the previous ten years, in continuation of my enquiries on the subject of the Polynesians and their history and migrations. Among other works on that subject which I had consulted in the colony, and from which I had made extracts, was the work of a learned Spanish writer, Martinez de Zuniga, entitled *Historia de las Islas Philipinas,* or a History of the Philippine Islands. In that work the Spaniard had advanced and advocated the singular hypothesis that, as the South Sea Islanders could never have made their way to the eastward across the Pacific Ocean in the face of the easterly trade winds of that ocean, the multitude of the Isles of the great South Sea must have been originally discovered and settled by emigrants from the West Coast of America. Without attaching the slightest importance to this hypothesis, which I considered from the first utterly untenable, yet, as the Spaniard had alleged in support of it that a striking conformity subsisted between the Indian language of Chili—from which he had derived a few specimens from the work of Erçilla, the Spanish historian of Chili—and that of the province of Tagala in the Philippine Islands, it seemed to me that if such a conformity really subsisted between these languages, it might be owing rather to an emigration of Polynesians to America than of Americans to Polynesia. The circumstances in which I happened to be placed at the moment were remarkably favourable for pursuing the train of thought into which I had thus been unexpectedly led. We were traversing the Southern Pacific, and approaching, at only a few degrees to the southward, the meridian of Easter Island—that remote and solitary isle, in which the colossal remains of a long extinct Polynesian civilization still prove beyond all controversy that this ancient race had reached and occupied that island during the period in which their long extinct civilization was a living and powerfully-active reality. And as I could not but recollect at the moment that, in my own previous and then recent voyage across the Pacific, our good ship had been carried during a violent westerly gale of upwards of four weeks' continuance, into that very neighbourhood on our way to Cape Horn, it struck me all at once with such force that I started up involuntarily in my cabin at the idea of having got upon the right track at last for the solution of the grand problem of this volume—the original discovery of America. For I saw at once that, if such a violent westerly gale as I had myself experienced only three years before, had caught a Polynesian vessel off the coast of Easter Island during the period of its ancient civilization, it would have carried her without fail across the remaining tract of ocean, and thereby given its first inhabitants to the Continent of America.

> How swift is a glance of the mind!
> Compared with the speed of its flight,
> The tempest itself lags behind,
> And the swift-winged arrows of light.*

That momentary glance of the mind in my own case convinced me that I had at length got upon the right track for the solution of the great mystery which had been hidden from mankind from the days of Columbus, and for the solution of which hundreds of different works had been written in vain—in English, in French, and in Spanish—I mean, THE ORIGINAL DISCOVERY AND PROGRESSIVE SETTLEMENT OF THE CONTINENT OF AMERICA.

Having, therefore, nothing further to do with De Zuniga, I set myself to test and verify, as far as it was possible to do so on shipboard and far at sea, what I could not help regarding from the first as a great discovery. With this view I proceeded, as is done in the *Rule of False* in arithmetic, by assuming a fact and then reasoning from it to ascertain its reality; or, as in algebra, by repre-

---

\* Cowper.

senting some unknown quantity by the letter $x$, and ascertaining from the conditions of the case what that quantity is.

The first question, therefore, that presented itself for enquiry in the case was, to what point on the West Coast of America would a Polynesian vessel caught suddenly, when off the coast of Easter Island, in a violent westerly gale, such as I had myself experienced in the year 1830,* be driven by the tempest? and the second was—in what directions would the unfortunate Polynesians proceed in their subsequent migrations, after effecting a settlement in the unknown land. As to the first of these questions, I was at once constrained to conclude that the unfortunate Polynesians must have landed somewhere near Copiapo, in what is now the State

---

\* The case of the Apostle Paul, when his good ship was caught suddenly in the tempest Euroclydon off the Island of Clauda, in the Mediterranean, will doubtless recur to the reader as somewhat parallel to the one supposed. I happened to pass in sight of that island on my return to New South Wales in the P. & O. Company's Branch Mail Steam Ship from Venice to Alexandria, in December, 1874, and naturally gazed at it in the distance with intense interest.

of Chili, in South America, in latitude 27° south, nearly; for the violence of the gale supposed would prevent them from diverging either north or south from the parallel of Easter Island. The second question I answered by shewing that they must have migrated either north or south, as the vicinity of the Andes would prevent them from getting far to the eastward.

Having settled these questions satisfactorily, as I conceived, I proceeded to enquire whether the architectural remains which these wanderers had doubtless left behind them in their subsequent migrations, bore any resemblance to those of the extinct civilization of Polynesia; whether there was any identity or resemblance in the singular manners and customs of the Indo-Americans and those of the South Sea Islanders; and, lastly, whether the languages of these two races of men gave any evidences of their common origin. In all these important points, the discussion of which occupies a large portion of this volume, I was fully satisfied that I was right in my theory; and, in order that so great an historical and ethnological discovery should neither be concealed from the world on the one hand, nor pirated on the other, I resolved to publish a small work on the subject, which I did, accordingly, in London, in the year 1834, under the same title as that of this volume, only prefixing the first words " A view of," &c., which my present publisher has dispensed with. This work, although, I acknowledge, a very imperfect production, as compared with the present volume, was very favourably reviewed in the Royal Geographical Society's journal of the day, as well as by two influential American reviews. But, while it was treated with much courtesy in the first of these quarters, and with absolute scepticism in the others; and while my theory was generally ridiculed by not a few able editors of the day as a perfect absurdity, further evidence, I found, was desired in certain other quarters before the great question, involved in the case, could be supposed to be finally settled. Such evidence I have now collected, after an interval of more than forty years, and beg to submit to the public.

I had not been mistaken in supposing that some attempt would have been made to appropriate my views and conclusions in regard to the Polynesians and their migrations, had I not published my book on the subject—the first edition of this work—in the year 1834. But that book was scarcely *out* when such an attempt was actually made, notwithstanding, in the very last quarter in which I could ever have expected it. For in the year 1835 or 1836 the Rev. John Williams, afterwards "the martyr of Erromanga," published his famous work, entitled "A Narrative of Missionary Enterprises in the South Sea Islands," which was so highly popular at the time that it had already reached the sixth thousandth in 1837. But my unfortunate book of two hundred pages, with all my arguments and conclusions—a work of great labour and research, and the result of much previous study, both on land and at sea — had, in the meantime, been actually compressed by Mr. Williams into ten or twelve pages of his "Narrative," *without one syllable of acknowledgment as to how or where they had come from.* In short, it was one of the most flagrant pieces of literary piracy I have ever known! I do not blame Mr. Williams so much, however, for this unwarrantable proceeding, so deeply fraught with injustice to myself. Mr. Williams, although one of Nature's own undoubted noblemen, was an uneducated man, and a mere working blacksmith, when he entered into the service of the London Missionary Society. But the Rev. William Ellis, the author of the work entitled " Polynesian Researches," which I have quoted so frequently in this volume, and afterwards the Apostle of Madagascar, was the Secretary of that Society at the time, and had all the literary work of its agents and servants on his hands. Mr. Williams merely supplied the facts, and Mr. Ellis wrought them up into a noble volume, which many good people at the time used to say was like a second volume of the Acts of the Apostles. But Mr. Ellis, being a literary man, and of much experience in connection with the Press, had doubtless told Mr. Williams that there was no necessity for any personal acknowledgment to me, in merely embodying in his own work the sum and substance of mine, especially as I was then out of the country and far away at the ends of the earth.

Besides, Mr. Ellis would doubtless suggest that the incorporation of my work would serve to make Mr. Williams' " Narrative " complete, by showing who the Polynesians were and where they came from, as also how they managed to find their way to the eastward across the broadest part of the Pacific, against the easterly trade winds of that ocean, not to mention, the little fact— that the Indo-Americans were so like the Polynesians, that it might be taken for granted, without saying anything more about it, that they came from the South Seas. Thus the three great points of my book of 1834, the fruit of ten years occasional study and research, both by land and sea, were literally *stolen* by Mr. Ellis to complete and embellish Mr. Williams' "Narrative," and thereby to do me an immense wrong. It would be a comparatively easy task for Mr. Ellis in such circumstances, to add a few particulars to what I had stated to throw unlearned people " off the scent." This accordingly was done freely.

Mr. Williams visited Sydney, on his return to the Islands towards the close of the year 1838. I called on him on the occasion, and as I understood that he was then looking out for a suitable place in our city for holding a large public meeting, for the benefit of his mission, I offered him the use of the Scots Church, which was then the largest building in Sydney available for such a purpose, and which had been used shortly before for a similar object, in honour of King George, the native King of the Tonga or Friendly Islands. Mr. Williams, however, did not accept my offer on returning my call, for what reason I could not divine at the time, for I had not then read his book; but I could not help observing, during his visit, that he had something on his mind that prevented him from holding more intimate relations with myself. He had, then, doubtless, recognized the extreme impropriety, to say the least of it, of his own proceeding in assenting to Mr. Ellis's suggestion in regard to the use he had made of my book. From what I recollect of the way in which that book (of 1834) had been used up in the first edition of Mr. Williams' "Narrative," which I only read on board ship, on my way to England, in the year 1839, I am of opinion that that portion of the work had been considerably modified by Mr. Ellis in the subsequent editions; but, as I have been unable to find any copy of the work in this colony of an earlier date than that of the sixth thousand, in 1837, I cannot state positively whether it was so or not. The fact, however, if it should ever be deemed a matter of importance, as it is likely to be now, can easily be ascertained in London by a reference to both works in the Library of the British Museum—mine of 1834, and Mr. Williams' first edition of 1835 or 1836.

In the meantime, the following extract from Mr. Ellis's own statements in the latest edition I have seen of his Polynesian researches, will shew how entirely his views had been changed after the publication of my book in 1834.

" The origin of the inhabitants of the Pacific,"

says Mr. Ellis, " is involved in great mystery, and the evidences are certainly strongest in favour of their derivation from the Malayan tribes inhabiting the Asiatic Islands; but, allowing this to be their source, the means by which they have arrived at the remote and isolated stations they now occupy, are still inexplicable. If they were peopled from the Malayan Islands, they must have possessed better vessels, and more accurate knowledge of navigation than they now exhibit, to have made their way against the constant trade-winds prevailing within the tropics, and blowing regularly, with but transient and uncertain interruptions, from east to west." Again—" On the other hand, it is easy to imagine how they could have proceeded from the east. The winds would favour their passage, and the incipient stages of civilization in which they were found would resemble the condition of the aborigines of America, far more than that of the Asiatics. There are many well-authenticated accounts of long voyages performed in native vessels by the inhabitants of both the North and

South Pacific. In 1696, two canoes were driven from Ancarso to one of the Philippine Islands, a distance of 800 miles. They had run before the wind for 70 days together, sailing from east to west." And again—" If we suppose the population of the South Sea Islands to have proceeded from east to west, these events illustrate the means by which it may have been accomplished; for it is a striking fact, that every such voyage related in the accounts of voyagers, preserved in the traditions of the natives, or of recent occurrence, has invariably been from east to west, directly opposite to that in which it must have been, had the population been altogether derived from the Malayan archipelago."*

Such, then, were what may be styled *the last words* of Mr. Ellis about the Pacific Ocean, after his own long residence in the Pacific, both north and south. That ocean was then just as great a mystery to him as it had been to others. The Polynesians were doubtless somewhat like

\* Polynesian Researches, Vol. I., pages 125 to 127.

the Malays, but how they could ever have crossed the Pacific in the face of the easterly trade winds of the intertropical regions, no man could divine. Besides, the Polynesians were just as like the Aboriginal Americans as they were to the Malays, and the passage from the east, across the Pacific, would merely be a run before the wind the whole way, as De Zuniga had urged. Such, then, was all the light Mr. Ellis had been able, to throw, in his conclusions, upon the mystery of the Pacific Ocean, when he had reached the close of his " Researches," and was publishing the second edition of his book, in the year 1831.

But the scene is altogether changed with him after the publication of my book, in 1834. To his great mortification, doubtless, he there finds that I had solved the two great problems of the Pacific Ocean, by tracing the Polynesians to their Malayan origin on the one hand, and by shewing, from La Perouse, Admiral Hunter, and other eminent navigators on the other, that it was quite as practicable, within certain latitudes and at certain seasons, to cross the Pacific from west to east as from east to west. He now alleges that there was no difficulty in the case at all, and that crossing the Pacific to the eastward was all a matter of plain sailing. Thus, by those figures of speech, which logicians call *suppressio veri* and *suggestio falsi* (concealing the truth and suggesting a falsehood), he ignores me altogether in the matter, and makes Mr. Williams assume the entire merit of my discoveries; thereby depriving me, in the estimation of the public, of the credit and the honour, for forty years past; for I have never taken any public notice of the grievous wrong thus done me until now.

I shall doubtless be told that my allusions to those eminent men, Mr. Ellis and Mr. Williams, who are now both long since dead, are in violation of the good old maxim, *De mortuis nil nisi bonum;* but history of any kind could never be written on that maxim; and the form which the maxim itself should assume, in all such cases, is *De mortuis nil nisi verum,* "say nothing of the dead but what is true."

For my own part, I deeply regret having been virtually compelled to mention these humiliating particulars in the case of two such men as Mr. Ellis and Mr. Williams; but independently of my own invaded rights in the matter, which surely deserved to be mentioned, the question as to the way in which the original discovery of the continent of America was effected by man, is of too world-wide an interest to allow any of the more important facts and circumstances connected with it to be concealed, whomsoever the mention of them may affect.

The three characteristic features of my book of 1834, as distinct from anything that Mr. Ellis, the author of the "Polynesian Researches," had ever previously published on the subject of Polynesia, were—first, " My successful identification of the Polynesians with the inhabitants of Eastern Asia and the Malays of the Indian Archipelago; " second, " My demonstration of the practicability of crossing the Pacific to the eastward, which I had established on evidence the most satisfactory, notwithstanding the easterly trade winds of the intertropical regions of that ocean;" and, third, " My discovery of the way and the means by which America had been first reached by the Polynesians, and their identification, as being the same people, with the Indo-Americans."

These three principles, the discovery and establishment of which had cost me much labour and research during the ten years of my previous residence in New South Wales, Mr. Ellis, the real author of Williams' " Narrative," appropriated wholesale in chapter 29th of that Narrative, page 503, without ever mentioning my name, or making me the slightest acknowledgment; thereby making Mr. Williams, who, in a literary point of view, stood to Mr. Ellis in much the same relations as his man Friday did to Robinson Crusoe, solely responsible for his own downright theft.

The way in which this felonious appropriation of my literary property was effected by the two joint-stock operators was as ingenious, and in much the same style, as any London burglary. After stating, for instance, in page 504 of the

"Narrative," as I had done in the outset of my book, that the South Sea Islands were inhabited by two distinct races of Polynesians, the eastern and the western, or the lighter coloured and the darker — the brown and the black — Mr. Ellis, *alias* Mr. Williams, goes on as follows: "The point, then, for consideration, is the origin of these Islanders. In tracing that of the copper-coloured Polynesians, *I find no difficulty.*" This is a remarkable statement on the part of Mr. Ellis, for, until after the publication of my book, in 1834, he had always found such insurmountable difficulty in tracing the origin of the Polynesians, that he had actually held and advocated the irrational theory of De Zuniga, that they had come from the continent of America, running down to the westward with the easterly fair wind. "Thus, I think," continues the writer of the "Narrative," "every difficulty is removed, and that we need not have recourse to the theory advocated by some writers, and countenanced to a certain extent by Mr. Ellis," — that is, by himself — "that the Polynesian islanders came from South America. Their physical conformation, their general character, and their Malay countenance, furnish, I think, indubitable evidence of their Asiatic origin. But to these proofs must be added the near affinity between the *caste* of India and the *tabu* of the South Sea Isles.* The similarity of opinions which prevailed respecting women, and the treatment they received in Polynesia and Bengal, more especially the common practice of forbidding them to eat certain kinds of food, or to partake of any in the presence of the men— their inhuman conduct to the sick—the immolation of the wives at the funeral of their husbands— and a great number of games and usages ;—these, I think, are clear indications of the Asiatic origin of this people: but the correspondence between the language spoken by the Malays and the Polynesians is a still more decisive evidence. Many

---

\* This was a slight mistake on the part of the dishonest copyist of my book. I had not alleged that there was any affinity between the Indian institution of caste and that of taboo in Polynesia. They have no connection with each other, but they exist alike both in India and in Polynesia.

of the words are the same in all the dialects of the South Sea Islands."

Now, these items are all the mere heads of my argument in proving the identity of the Polynesians, first with the natives of India, and then with the Malays; and the six words which Mr. Ellis cites in the "Narrative" to prove the identity of the Polynesian and Malayan languages are the identical six which I had cited for the same purpose in my book. They are as follows:—

| English. | Malay. | Polynesian. |
|---|---|---|
| The eye | Mata | Mata |
| Food | Mangan | Manga |
| Dead | Maté | Maté |
| A bird | Manu | Manu |
| Fish | Ika | Ika |
| Water | Vai | Vai. |

"Thus, I think," Mr. Ellis proceeds in Mr. Williams' "Narrative," "I have disposed of the first objection *to my theory*, and I now proceed to the consideration of the second—the prevalence of the easterly trade winds. This has been by many a conclusive argument against the Asiatic origin of the South Sea Islanders, but I do not attach to it so much importance."

The fact is, Mr. Ellis never had a theory on the subject of crossing the Pacific from the westward in the face of the easterly trade winds of that ocean. So far was he from anything of the kind—from thinking even that the thing was possible—that, by his own confession, he stuck to the theory of De Zuniga, that the South Sea Islands were peopled from America, until after the publication of my book in 1834. *Then*, indeed, he changed his tune at once, when he found that I had demonstrated the practicability of crossing the Pacific from the westward, notwithstanding the easterly trade winds; for immediately after his own confession of his abandonment of the Spaniard's theory, he adds, " *I would far rather say*, provided the physical conformation, the structure of their language, and other circumstances established the identity of the Polynesians and the aborigines of America, *that the latter reached that continent through the Isles of the Pacific.*" Now, Mr. Ellis never had the slightest idea of the Polynesians having reached

America in their wonderful migrations until after the publication of my book. But when he there found that I had not only suggested the idea, and shown the very point of departure for the Polynesians in their last and most remarkable migration, from Easter Island to America, but had actually proved the identity of the Polynesians and the Indo-Americans, from their architectural remains, their manners and customs, and various other circumstances, he again virtually adopts my idea, although, in order to prevent me from getting any credit for it, he claims it as his own, and professes to suggest the grand idea of the aborigines of America *having reached that continent through the isles of the Pacific.*

Now, my dear Mr. Ellis, this was the *unkindest cut of all!* After robbing me of the product of my brain, the dearest article of property that a literary man can possess, by appropriating my two great discoveries of the origin and earlier movements of the Polynesian race, and the practicability of crossing the Pacific from the westward, notwithstanding the prevalence of the easterly trade winds in the intertropical regions of that ocean—you endeavour to rob me, also, as you have been doing with some success for forty years past, of the credit of having been the original and the only discoverer of God's way of peopling America, after man had been vainly toiling at the great problem in all the languages of Europe for upwards of three centuries before.

It is somewhat singular that, after his very exceptional procedure towards myself as a brother author and a brother minister, in the matter in question, Mr. Ellis—for I make no account of Mr. Williams, his humble fellow-worker, in the case—should not have taken some better means than he did of shielding himself from public reprobation, if the fact should ever come to be known, as it certainly will now. For example, in referring in the introduction of my book to the nature of the investigation on which it proposed to enter, I had stated that " it promised to open up the darkest and the most mysterious portion of the ancient history of man. But Mr. Ellis makes use of these very words in his own remarks on the subject, observing that "This, indeed, is a dark and mysterious chapter in the history of man," as if he wished it to be known that he had got the sentiment from me.

Mr. Ellis also makes two quotations about the Malays in Mr. Williams' "Narrative"—the one from Mr. Marsden's "History of Sumatra," and the other from "Captain (afterwards Admiral) King's Voyages along the North Coast of Australia"—two rather out-of-the-way books; but it is remarkable enough that both of these quotations had been previously made in my book.

For my own part, I have never known so gross an instance of literary piracy as that of Mr. Ellis towards myself in the 29th chapter of Mr. Williams' "Narrative of Missionary Enterprises in the South Sea Islands"—a work of which Mr. Ellis, at the time, as Secretary of the London Missionary Society, superintended the publication, if he was not rather the real author. It was not a case of mere ordinary plagiarism; it was robbing me, as far as he could, of the credit of not fewer than three distinct discoveries I had made in the South

Seas—the last of which, that of the way in which the original discovery and progressive settlement of America had been effected through some unfortunate Polynesian vessel having been driven off Easter island by some violent gale of westerly wind, and carried across the intervening tract of ocean to the American land—this I regard as one of the greatest literary discoveries of the present age.

In calling at the University of Sydney a few weeks since, to borrow one of the immense folio volumes of Lord Kingsborough's "Monuments of Mexico," to get a copy of a drawing of an ancient Mexican temple as a frontispiece for this volume, the Registrar of the University observed, in conversation on my forthcoming volume, that my idea of deriving the Indo-Americans from the South Sea Islands was not an original one, as he had seen it elsewhere repeatedly. It was first announced to the world, however, in my book of 1834, in which I not only showed how the Polynesians must have crossed the intervening tract of ocean from Easter Island to America, under a violent gale of westerly wind, but proved, as I conceive, the identity of the Polynesian and Indo-American people. But that book was pirated very shortly thereafter, and I have been unjustly deprived of the credit and the honour of my discovery for forty years past. At all events the idea and the discovery it implied were wholly and exclusively mine.

Ever since the publication of my very imperfect work on the subject of this volume in the year 1834, I had determined, if Divine Providence should grant me life and health for the purpose, to publish a second edition, as I now do, after the lapse of upwards of forty years, with all the additional evidence I could collect in the interval, to prove my theory that, through one of those accidents that have doubtless been of constant occurrence throughout the vast Pacific Ocean for three or four thousand years past, and that have served from time to time during that long period to people the multitude of the isles, a mere handful of Polynesians—fishing, perhaps, off the coast of Easter Island in the Southern Pacific—had been suddenly caught by a violent gale of westerly wind, and carried across the intervening tract of ocean to the American land, landing somewhere near Copiapo in the state of Chili, in South America; and that the descendants of these Polynesian unfortunates, carrying with them the long extinct but comparatively high civilization of the South Sea Islands in long ages past, had, in the course of many succeeding generations, progressively settled the whole of the continent of America from Cape Horn to Labrador.

As a believer in Divine Revelation, I hold also that God not only made the earth to be inhabited, but that, in order to the fulfilment of that Divine purpose in regard to America, He planted that remote and solitary isle, Pasquas or Easter Island, in the deep sea exactly where it stands for the express purpose of serving as a stepping-stone for people of the Polynesian race to reach America; and I regard myself highly honoured by Divine Providence in having been selected to solve the great problem that has vainly exercised the ingenuity of the learned of all European nations ever since the days of Columbus, or for upwards of three centuries past, in demonstrating how that continent was originally discovered and settled, and in therefore proving to the satisfaction, I believe, of all intelligent and candid persons that God had made of one blood both the Polynesian and Indo-American nations, and that all the efforts of modern scepticism to prove the latter a distinct creation, or the mere result of evolution, are therefore as silly and futile as they are uncalled for.

---

*By the same Author*,

AN HISTORICAL AND STATISTICAL ACCOUNT OF NEW SOUTH WALES, FROM THE FOUNDING OF THE COLONY IN 1788, TO THE PRESENT DAY.

*Fourth Edition.*

IN TWO VOLUMES, 8VO. PRICE, ONE GUINEA.

London: Sampson, Low, and Co.
1875.

---

GIBBS, SHALLARD, AND CO., Printers, Pitt Street, Sydney.

www.ingramcontent.com/pod-product-compliance
Lightning Source LLC
Chambersburg PA
CBHW030000240426
43672CB00007B/768